English in plain words

WRITING I

English in plain words

A Composition & Language Program for High School Based on *Plain English Please* and *Background for Writing*

WRITING I

GREGORY COWAN

ELISABETH McPHERSON

RANDOM HOUSE / SINGER SCHOOL DIVISION
RANDOM HOUSE, INC., NEW YORK

SCHOOL EDITION PUBLISHED 1971
Copyright © 1966, 1969, 1971 by Random House, Inc.
Published in the United States by Random House, Inc., New York, and
simultaneously in Canada by Random House of Canada Limited, Toronto.

International Standard Book Number: 394-02450-8
Manufactured in the United States of America
171.1

CONTENTS

INTRODUCTION

ENGLISH IN PLAIN WORDS is a straightforward, practical, and relaxed way to study English. The program is designed to improve your writing and heighten your awareness of how the writing system works.

The composition books, *Writing I* and *Writing II*, give experience in writing for particular purposes, such as explaining, giving directions, and persuading. These are practical writing tasks encountered in the everyday world. Whatever you do after high school, you will have to be competent in them. The composition books emphasize clear thinking, for clear thinking is essential for clear writing.

The two language books, *Sounds and Letters* and *Words*, take a common sense approach to language history, phonology, the dictionary, and grammar and show how the talking system of English relates to the writing system.

Practical Helps offers assistance with problems of punctuation, library research, and certain conventional writing forms.

ENGLISH IN PLAIN WORDS begins with the assumption that you already know far more about how English works than this or any other book can teach you. It's your language. You're an expert in using it. When you learned to talk, before you even started school, you learned to master a complex system. The proof of your mastery is that you can understand what other speakers of English say to you—at least most of the time—and they can understand you. But in a literate society talking is not enough. What you studied in school was not the talking system but another system altogether, a system for recording talk, the writing system. In the last ten or twelve years, you've read a lot of books and you've written a lot of papers. But all that time you kept on talking. We all talk probably a hundred times as much as we write. With all that practice it's small wonder that most of us feel more comfortable talking.

The difficulties we sometimes have with writing, however, result from more than just lack of practice. Although writing is a system for making talk "permanent," effective writing is always more than talk written down. ENGLISH IN PLAIN WORDS helps you understand what these differences are and offers some practical ways of coping with them. The program helps you recognize what makes good writing good and gives you a chance to practice what you learn. The program may not make you into a Chomsky or a Hemingway, but it will improve your understanding, skill, and effectiveness. You should become almost as comfortable writing as you already are talking.

Writing I examines one reason for any kind of communication—explaining what you mean. Talking an idea out of your head and into someone else's is one thing; writing it is quite another. If you understand some of the differences between a spoken explanation and a written one, you can probably make your written explanations much more effective.

In conversation several things are going on, and communication of information is only one of them. Talking is a social custom, a way of filling time. If we like the people we're talking to, we may take as much pleasure in their voices and their presence as in what gets said. If we're indifferent to them, or even dislike them, we may use talking as an outlet for other emotions, our frustration or our fury. But however we feel about the people we're talking to, there's still another element: we want to look good, to them and to ourselves. So even when we concentrate on making ourselves clear, the explanation itself is only one of our purposes.

Another more obvious difference between spoken and written explanations lies in the clues the listener gives us by his gestures and his facial expressions. A slight frown, an almost invisible shake of his head, can show us that we're not getting through. Those clues warn us to repeat, give more details, change our approach, or ask what the trouble is. We answer the listener's questions, perhaps ask some of our own. We don't use a definite plan because what we say and the order we follow both depend on the clues we pick up. At the same time, we're giving out clues of our own: we demonstrate with our hands, we raise and lower our voices, we pause to let a point sink in, we smile and scowl and sigh.

When we write our explanations, however, not only are these double sets of clues missing, but most of the other purposes have dropped out too. We may still want to impress—most of us always want to do that—but usually when we take the trouble to write our explanations, we want our work to pay off in greater clarity. Because we know our readers may be 100 feet or 100 miles away, because we know they may be reading ten minutes or ten days after we write, we must be more deliberate about recognizing our purpose and sticking to it. We must anticipate their clues and compensate for ours by more careful organization, more complete development, more conscious transitions.

No writer will take such pains, however, unless he is convinced that the writing he does represents a sensible human activity, undertaken for a definite reason. In this book we have tried to make the writing assignments "real," to suggest topics and occasions which actually need explanations. If the topics at the end of the chapters don't challenge you, find some that do and share them with the class. If you can see a better way of achieving your purpose than the plans suggested here, share those ideas too. This is your course, your book, your language; make it fit your needs.

I

Finding the Purpose

Before you begin to write anything, no matter what it is—a check for $42.98, a petition to keep the school cafeteria open later, a letter to the editor opposing the draft—you need to ask yourself, "Why am I writing this? What do I hope to accomplish?" Sometimes the answer is obvious: you are writing the check to keep the collection agency from collecting your car. You are writing the petition because you get hungry after a long day of classes. You are opposing the draft because you want to convince other people that the present system is unfair and perhaps because you want to see your ideas in print.

It may seem to you that the reason for writing an English paper is some-what different, though equally obvious: the teacher assigned it, and you have no choice. You are writing it because you *have* to. But if you stop to think a minute, you will see that the reason for writing an English paper is not much different from the basic reason behind all writing; it *has* to be done so that the writer will get something he wants. Almost no sane person writes for the pleasure of setting words on paper one after the other. Did you ever hear anybody say, "Goody, goody, I *get* to write a letter tonight"? The natural phrase is "I *have* to write a letter," and the "have" implies, as usual, that the writing is being done, not for its own sake, but because the writer expects some reward or satisfaction, however small, from the thing he has written.

The statement that nobody writes for the fun of it applies just as much to professional writers as it does to students. The professional writer may take pleasure in thinking about what he has written, if he thinks it turned out well; but the actual writing is work, not fun. Homer has left no record of the agony he went through in composing the *Odyssey*, but we do know that the manager of the Globe Theatre was always nagging Shakespeare to finish that fifth act by Friday night. In the last hundred years or so, nearly every writer who has analyzed the process of writing has talked about the sweat and strain that go into every paragraph. From Charles Dickens, who spent sleepless nights grinding out another chapter to meet a magazine deadline, to Dorothy Parker, who, it is said, was so desperately anxious to avoid facing the blank sheet of paper in her typewriter that—to encourage visitors—she hung a sign saying "Gentlemen" on her office door, professional writers agree in saying that they did not write for fun.

Just as Charles Dickens (and even Dorothy Parker, when the gentlemen had gone on back to their own offices) wrote to get the money for the grocery bill, so other writers force themselves to write because they must. Most registered nurses would rather bathe the accident victim in ward seven than write out careful directions on how to give the bath. But the student nurse who comes on at ten o'clock will need the directions. Most engineers would rather build another bridge than write an explanation of what went wrong with pier seven. But the company demands to know why the pier fell down. Hardly anybody who is shaken and bruised from a collision enjoys writing a report of the accident for the highway patrol and the insurance adjuster. Most teachers would rather read another book than summarize what their colleagues said at the conference. A worried college freshman may not get much fun out of writing home for that extra ten dollars he just must have.

All these people write because they believe something desirable will result from their writing. The nurse believes that her careful directions may spare the patient some unnecessary pain. The engineer wants to make it clear that the bridge collapse was not his fault. The owner of the smashed Volkswagen and the stiff neck hopes to get his car repaired and avoid having his driver's license revoked. The teacher hopes his department head will send him to another conference. And the freshman, of course, expects to get his hands on that ten by return mail.

All these writers know, first, that they have to write. But more important, they know *why* they have to write. They have a clear understanding of their purpose, and they are not likely to be sidetracked into forgetting it. The nurse is not likely to break off her directions for turning the patient on his side to complain about the coffee served in the hospital dining room. The engineer is not likely to interrupt his discussion of the strength of concrete mixes to argue against American policy in the Far East. The accident report will contain no comments on how hot it was at the beach or how plentiful the fish were last Saturday. If the teacher at the conference breaks off his summary of Dr. Philpot's analysis of *The Poetics* to tell about the funny thing that happened on the way to his hotel room, he will probably not be sent to the conference next year—unless he can make his story at once very funny and very relevant. Nor is the boy whose aim is to get ten dollars likely to fill his letter home with a glowing description of the daffodils outside his door—unless his mother is mad about daffodils and he thinks he can establish some connection between the flowers that bloom in the spring, tra-la, and his urgent need to loosen the family purse strings. The chances for success in writing are always greater if the writer understands his purpose clearly and keeps that purpose firmly in mind all the time he is writing.

Giving Directions

Let's look at a few purposes that make people abandon their natural sluggishness and set pen to paper. One common purpose is to tell other people how to do something, to give directions. That was what the registered nurse was doing. That was what the doctor did when he left the original set of instructions for the nurse. That is what the makers of TV dinners do on their containers—and the makers of dress patterns, and house paints, and do-it-yourself kits of all kinds. Whenever anybody offers step-by-step advice on completing any kind of project, he is giving directions.

Explaining

Another common purpose is to explain something. In one sense, of course, the nurse and the doctor and the dress pattern manufacturers are *explaining* to their readers what steps to follow in tending patients and making clothes. Their purpose, however, is to speak directly to somebody who will be actually doing something rather than just trying to understand something. The writer who is giving directions is saying, "Do this, then do that." The writer making other kinds of explanation deals with meaning or relationships, and he never talks to his readers as though he were giving commands. Almost all the differences between giving directions and other kinds of explaining are shown in the differences between:

Take off your shoes before you come into the living room.

and

A polite Japanese removes his shoes before he comes into a house, just as automatically and naturally as an American removes his top-coat and his overshoes.

Or between:

Don't stick bobby pins into an electric outlet.

and

Electric current at 110 volts can cause a shock severe enough to injure a small child.

Although giving directions is often very reasonably considered one kind of explanation, the way directions are written is different enough from the way other explanations are written that we will consider directions a separate writing purpose and save the term *explanation* for the kind of writing that defines or compares or classifies or analyzes.

For instance, the engineer is *explaining* the technical reasons behind the collapse of pier seven into the Po-Po River, taking with it thirty-seven workmen who didn't want a bath. The college catalog you will receive from the registrar next summer is designed to *explain* admission and graduation requirements. Here are some other examples of explanation:

Anthropology is the study of man's physical and cultural characteristics.

The cottontail differs from the jackrabbit in several important ways.

Rats, mice, and rabbits belong to the rodent family.

In order to understand the working of a threshing machine, we must consider each of its separate parts.

Many elementary texts, in science or in English, for instance, are made up of explanation. Part of what we are doing in this chapter is explaining the difference between one writing purpose and another.

Telling What Happened

Some occasions call not for explanation but for telling what happened. The accident report, if it is to serve its purpose, must contain no analysis of the unrestrained, illegal, inconsiderate, nincompoopish nature of the other driver's driving habits. It must contain no directions as to just where that other driver ought to go. Instead, it must be limited to a clear and complete account of just what occurred.

Newspaper articles are another example of writing that tells what happened. A front-page news story says, "Thirteen people were killed in weekend highway accidents," or "A severe earthquake left thousands homeless," or "The City Council passed a zoning ordinance last night." But newswriters do not, in their front-page accounts, warn you to drive carefully, or urge you to send sandwiches and blankets to the homeless, or tell you the council members are a pack of reactionary idiots. You may find these lectures and pleas and opinions on the editorial page or in syndicated columns, but the news story itself, like an accident report, will tell only what happened.

Convincing Others

Perhaps the commonest purpose is to try to get others to agree with you or to make them do what you want. The boy who wrote home for money was trying to convince his mother that he really needed that ten dollars more than she needed to keep it. Congressman Gruntansqueal's every written word is designed to convince the voters in his home district that he is the greatest statesman to hit the country since George Washington was laid to rest. Ad writers try to convince you that Twinkle toothpaste will make your teeth a whiter white, that Fatiac automobiles will cut your gasoline bill in half and double your community standing, and that Vital Vitamins will make you captain of the football team. When you sit in church on Sunday, the sermon is designed to convince you that you should mend your wicked ways, or, if your ways are not wicked, that you should love your fellow man. When you were little, your parents tried to convince you that a good child picks up his toys and does not hit his brother with a baseball bat. From the minute you started school your teachers tried to convince you that education is a fine and useful thing.

Summarizing

Another common purpose is to summarize what someone else has written. The teacher who shortened Dr. Philpot's twenty-four pages of remarks to a single page was summarizing. And so was the editorial assistant who shortened the teacher's page to three brief sentences, muttering all the while about the windiness of old age. Some digest magazines have made millions of dollars and gained millions of readers by hacking long articles into shorter ones. When you take your finals at the end of a course, you are compressing into four or five pages of writing what you think the content of the course has been. In short, a summary is any piece of writing that shortens another piece of writing, without changing its meaning or commenting on it.

Exercise 1. Which purpose (giving directions, explaining, telling what happened, summarizing, or convincing) is expressed in each of these sentences? Notice that you are not being asked whether you think the sentence would be a good main idea for a paper, but only to decide what its purpose is.

1. In 1941, Japan attacked Pearl Harbor. _____

2. Add an onion, a clove of garlic, and two tablespoonfuls of Italian seasoning; stir vigorously. _____

3. Success in college depends on four things: ability to read, ability to write, time enough for studying, and money enough for tuition. _____

4. All college students should be required to serve in the armed forces. _____

5. *Romeo and Juliet* is the story of two young people who loved each other in spite of the feud between their families. _____

6. Last week seventy students were initiated into the honor society. _____

7. The United States should use hydrogen bombs on Red China. _____

8. The United Nations should use hydrogen bombs on the United States. _____

9. The main idea expressed in Senator Hoaxshell's pamphlet was that crime and immorality must be stopped without costing the government any money. _____

10. Uncle Vanya fell into a manhole yesterday. _____

11. The city should be more careful about leaving manholes uncovered. _____

12. Manholes provide entrance to pipes under the street. _____

13. There aren't enough manholes in Mudville's main streets. _____

14. *V*, a book by Thomas Pynchon, tells about a man who worked for some time killing alligators in the sewers under New York City. _____

15. Most modern cities have installed sewage disposal systems. _____

16. The system in our town is hopelessly out of date. _____

17. Yesterday's *Morning Tattler* reported that seventy-five antennas had been broken off cars in Pittsburgh last week. _____

18. Vandalism must be stopped. _____

19. To insure greater safety, remove the keys and lock your car when you park it. _____

20. To find a book in the library, simply follow these steps. _____

Blending Purposes

The five purposes—giving directions, explaining things, telling what happened, convincing others, and summarizing—occur over and over again. Sometimes these purposes occur separately. But experienced writers know that to accomplish their main purpose, they may need to use more than one of these methods. Before a writer can *convince* you that eating seaweed is nutritious and economical, he may have to *explain* the dietary needs of the human body and the comparative cost of a yard of seaweed and a pound of steak. In order to *convince* you that you too can enjoy a seaweed soufflé, he may need to *tell* you *what happened* the first time he had seaweed for supper. His main purpose was to convince, but he used two other writing methods—explaining and telling what happened.

Before any writer can blend methods effectively, he must become skillful in using each method separately. Writing is a skill that can be learned. Like any other skill, it must be learned one step at a time. By working on each purpose separately, you can learn to give directions, to explain, to tell what happened, to convince, and to summarize. And when you need to blend purposes, you'll probably have a much better chance of keeping the emphasis where you want it.

Narrowing the Topic

Your teacher may make your first efforts easy by assigning a writing purpose and leaving the topic up to you. If he says, "Write a theme about something you believe in, trying to get other people to agree with you," you know your general purpose must be to convince.

On the other hand, your teacher may just assign a topic, leaving the choice of purpose up to you. If he simply says, "Write a paper on sports," you have to cut the topic down to size before you can decide on your purpose. Obviously, you can't give directions for sports in general. You can't explain all the sports in the world. You can't tell what happened in a game of "sports." And you can't very well be in favor of all the sports there are, or against them all, though you may very well prefer some sports to others.

As you narrow this extremely broad topic down to manageable size, be sure to choose a sport you know something about. Perhaps you are a baseball fan. But when you say, "My paper will be about baseball," you have not stated your purpose; you have only taken the first step in narrowing your topic. At last count there were 5,387,422 ways to talk about baseball. It is not enough to decide that you are going to say *something* about baseball; you must decide *what* you are going to say.

Exercise 2.　　　All of the topics listed below are too broad for a 500-word paper—or a 5000-word paper, for that matter. For each very broad topic, suggest 3 narrow topics. For instance, if you begin with the broad topic *War,* you might narrow it to:

WAR:　Causes of the American Revolution
　　　The GI in World War II
　　　The possibilities of disarmament
　　　Foot soldiers in Caesar's army
　　　The War of Jenkins' Ear
　　　What the White Paper says about Vietnam
　　　The gains made at the Battle of the Bulge
　　　What is a tactical victory?
　　　Fifteenth-century weapons
　　　Duties of a first sergeant in the U.S. Army

1. psychology　　　(1) _____

　　　　　　　　　(2) _____

　　　　　　　　　(3) _____

2. pets　　　　　　(1) _____

　　　　　　　　　(2) _____

　　　　　　　　　(3) _____

3. parents　　　　(1) _____

　　　　　　　　　(2) _____

　　　　　　　　　(3) _____

4. urban problems　(1) _____

　　　　　　　　　(2) _____

　　　　　　　　　(3) _____

5. travel　　　　　(1) _____

　　　　　　　　　(2) _____

　　　　　　　　　(3) _____

6. money

(1) _____

(2) _____

(3) _____

7. magazines

(1) _____

(2) _____

(3) _____

8. literature

(1) _____

(2) _____

(3) _____

9. patriotism

(1) _____

(2) _____

(3) _____

10. education

(1) _____

(2) _____

(3) _____

Finding a Main Idea Sentence

What could you say about the topic baseball? You might say:

1. Baseball builds character.
2. During Little League games, parents should fight only in the bleachers.
3. Louisville needs a new baseball park.
4. There are several reasons for the size and shape of a catcher's mitt.
5. Softball differs from baseball in several ways.
6. Raglan College defeated St. Trinian last night.
7. When I was dropped from the varsity team, I discovered it pays to follow directions.
8. To care for a baseball uniform properly, the player must follow seven distinct steps.
9. In his article in *The Baseball World* for August, 1884, Clive Strongney discusses the reasons for calling baseball a typically American sport.

These nine sentences have two things in common: first, they all further narrow the general topic of baseball, and second, they all suggest what the purpose of the paper will be. Numbers 1, 2, and 3 express the writer's opinion; his purpose will be to make his reader share his belief. Numbers 4 and 5 will lead to papers of explanation. Numbers 6 and 7 will tell what happened: number 6 should lead to an objective report, telling what happened in the game; number 7 should lead to telling what happened in a personal experience. Number 8 will be a paper giving directions; number 9 will be a summary. All nine of these sentences make clear, definite statements. They are not topics, but *main idea sentences*.

Before you begin to write any kind of paper, you should work out a main idea sentence for it. Your main idea sentence must make clear what the purpose of your paper will be, and it must state the idea or event on which your paper will be based. It must make this statement in the form of a *complete sentence.*

Certainly the statement "I am going to write about baseball" is, in the grammatical sense, a complete sentence. But the sentence that states your main idea must not contain such obvious evasions as "I am going to write about . . ." or "My paper will be about . . ." In testing for the completeness of your idea, you must strike out all such repetitions of the original question ("What are you writing about?") and examine what remains. After you have crossed out "I am going to write about" or "This paper will be about," do you still have a complete sentence? "Baseball" or "Playing baseball" or even "When I played baseball" or "Why I like baseball" are not complete sentences. "When I played baseball" leads to the question "What happened?" and "Why I like baseball" leads to "Why do you?" You have not stated your main idea clearly until you can say, "When I played baseball, I learned that too much practice can sometimes lead to defeat," or "I like baseball because I am good at it."

Check your main idea to make sure that it is not *too* narrow. "A baseball is round" is certainly a complete sentence, and so is "Our coach's name was Baby Ruth," but neither of them is a satisfactory main idea sentence. Once you have announced the fact, you are left with nothing else to say.

As you look at your main idea sentence, the things you could use to support it or complete it should suggest themselves easily. If your main idea sentence is "College baseball builds character," you might say that the players learn sportsmanship, teamwork, and good health habits. It will take you at least a paragraph for each of these subdivisions, and you will discover, as you begin to write, that you have plenty to say. In the same way, "Softball differs from baseball in several ways" calls for a paragraph on each of the major differences, and "To care for a baseball uniform properly, the player must follow seven distinct steps" calls for a paragraph on each of the seven steps. If, when you look at your main idea sentence, you cannot think of three or four paragraphs that would logically develop from it, discard that sentence and find another one.

Once you have your main idea clearly stated, the hard part, deciding what to write, is behind you. But if you begin to write without a clear main idea sentence, you will find yourself floundering. Like the disorganized gardener, you will reap chaos.

Even the most confused student understands the importance of stating his main idea clearly in things that really matter to him. He is unlikely to write:

> *Dear Mamma,*
> This letter is about money.
> *With love, your son,*
> Rupert Creech

and then think he has taken care of the situation.

Exercise 3.   Which of the following are clear statements of a main idea? Which are merely topics, expressed in such a way that you cannot tell what the main idea would be? Mark *M* for main idea, *T* for topic.

1. My most exciting weekend.   _____

2. This paper will be about flying airplanes.   _____

3. Jets are quite different from propeller-driven airplanes.   _____

4. Manufacturing aircraft is a major factor in the economic structure of many large cities.   _____

5. Airplanes.   _____

6. Telling how to fly airplanes.   _____

7. Stunt flying is exciting.   _____

8. Aviation safety regulations should be made more severe.   _____

9. Aviation safety regulations should be made less severe.   _____

10. Reading newspapers.   _____

11. Too much aspirin.   _____

12. Desdemona's role in *Othello*.   _____

13. Soccer.   _____

14. Camel racing is for jerks.   _____

15. Before you rebuild a grandfather clock, you will need three things.   _____

16. When I rebuilt our grandfather clock.   _____

17. Extracurricular activities at St. Trinian College.   _____

18. St. Trinian should clean up its extracurricular activities. _____

19. A book report on *Tinkerbell*.   _____

20. A summary of *Tinkerbell*.   _____

21. *Tinkerbell* is a true account of a solo trip across the Atlantic
    on a fifteen-foot sailboat.   _____

22. What I think of *Tinkerbell*.   _____

23. How to build a sailboat.   _____

24. Registering for the draft.   _____

25. What happened when I saw my draft board.   _____

26. The Washington peace march.   _____

27. Guns versus butter.   _____

28. The Republican party is divided into two distinct factions.   _____

29. This paper will be about the split in the Republican party.   _____

30. Dental technicians must follow a carefully outlined course of
    study.   _____

31. Why I want to be a dental technician.   _____

32. A dip-stick heater can be a convenient way of warming a car
    on a cold morning.   _____

33. I'm going to explain the effects of napalm.   _____

34. *Tight Little Island* is one of the funniest movies ever made.   _____

35. *Tight Little Island* tells what happens when a cargo of whiskey
    washes ashore on a little island off the British coast.   _____

36. The Suburban Transit Company of Greater Mudville.   _____

Exercise 4. Decide which of the following main idea sentences are too broad, which are too narrow, and which are suitable for a theme of 500 words. Mark *B* for broad, *N* for narrow, and *S* for satisfactory. Be prepared to explain your decisions to the class.

1. A-frame houses are practical for three reasons. _____

2. Building your own A-frame house is very easy if you follow these 273 simple steps. _____

3. There are several variations on the standard A-frame house and each has its individual advantages. _____

4. My uncle has an A-frame house. _____

5. My uncle is a nerd. _____

6. I have raised many different breeds of camels. _____

7. The history of urban planning in America began with the construction of Washington, D. C. in the early nineteenth century. _____

8. *The Oxford English Dictionary,* the most complete dictionary of any language ever compiled, is in ten volumes. _____

9. *The Oxford English Dictionary* gives a complete history of every English word from its first written appearance to the present. _____

10. *The Oxford English Dictionary* is a useful reference. _____

11. I chose my college dictionary for three reasons. _____

12. My copy of *Little Goody Two-Shoes* is bound in blue-checked gingham. _____

13. Last summer I took a bicycle trip through Norway, Sweden, Denmark, Finland, the Netherlands, Scotland, and the Isle of Man. _____

14. The dike system in the Netherlands is a great aid to agriculture. _____

15. I admired the wooden shoes I saw. _____

16. Sigmund Freud discovered the unconscious. _____

17. Freud's theory of psychoanalysis rests on the existence of the id, the ego, and the superego. _____

18. Every time I start to read Freud's *Interpretation of Dreams* I go to sleep. _____

19. Last night I had a long dream about being chased through the sewers of Paris by Jean Valjean. _____

20. Freud was born in Austria. _____

21. *Les Misérables* is one of the most fascinating books I have ever read. _____

22. *Les Misérables* is a very long book. _____

23. St. Louis, Missouri, is named for Louis IX of France. _____

24. New Orleans is on the Gulf of Mexico. _____

25. The Mardi gras is an exotic carnival held in New Orleans every spring. _____

26. Mardi gras means fat Tuesday. _____

27. I lost fifteen pounds during the last Mardi gras. _____

28. The development of American movies covers a period of more than fifty years. _____

29. *King Kong* is perhaps the most popular of all the movies ever made in which an ape played the male lead. _____

30. King Kong dies at the end of the movie. _____

Exercise 5. Write a possible statement of a main idea for each of the following topics. If the topic is too broad, narrow it before you write your main idea statement. For instance, the topic *sewing* might be narrowed to "method of hemming a dress," and then the main idea statement might be:

> Three acceptable ways to hem a dress are: straight machine sewing, blind stitching done by machine, and hand stitching. (explanation)

Or the broad topic *public officials* could be narrowed to "the Pleasantville Dogcatcher," and the main idea statement might be:

> The Pleasantville Dogcatcher has a very easy job. (convincing)

Name the purpose of each sentence (in parentheses, as in examples above). Try for some variety. Use each writing purpose at least once but not more than four times.

1. graduation requirements _____

_____

_____

2. marriage _____

_____

_____

3. police department _____

_____

_____

4. intermural sports _____

_____

_____

5. movies _____

_____

_____

6. hobbies _____

_____

_____

7. counselors _____

_____

_____

8. English class _____

_____

_____

9. construction _____

_____

_____

10. jobs _____

_____

_____

Exercise 6.   For each of the following topics, write:

    a. a main idea sentence for a paper giving directions;
    b. a main idea sentence for a paper of explanation;
    c. a main idea sentence for a paper telling what happened;
    d. a main idea sentence for a paper to convince.

Use your own paper. Label the purpose of each statement.
For instance, the topic *house fires* might lead to these main idea sentences:

GIVING DIRECTIONS: Even if you wake up some night to find smoke pouring out of the kitchen, you may be able to save the house if you do three things coolly and quickly.

EXPLAINING: The Home Fire Underwriters' Association lists the four most frequent causes of home fires.

TELLING WHAT HAPPENED: A four-story house in East Ignitia burned to the ground last night.

CONVINCING: Every home-owner should carry fire insurance.

1. student riots
2. rats
3. cigarettes
4. tennis shoes
5. plagiarism

Exercise 7.   Look in a newspaper to find five paragraphs, each illustrating a different kind of writing purpose. Try to avoid paragraphs using mixed purposes; you can find single purposes more easily if you clip only single paragraphs, rather than entire articles. Paste, staple, or tape your paragraphs to a sheet of notebook paper so they won't get lost if your instructor asks you to hand them in. Be sure to label the purpose of each paragraph.

Key Words

If you know exactly how these key words are used in the chapter, and if you can answer the questions about them, you can be fairly certain that you have understood the most important points made in the chapter. If you have difficulty with the questions, reread the chapter, keeping the questions in mind. Used conscientiously, this section can help you in two ways: it can be a handy review section to prepare you for tests, and it can help you read with attention to the main points.

1. A *topic* is . . .

2. *Narrowing a topic* means . . .

3. A *main idea sentence* is . . .

4. Finding your *writing purpose* means . . .

5. A piece of writing that *gives directions* is . . .

6. A piece of writing that *explains* tells . . .

7. A *report* tells only . . .

8. A *summary* should . . .

9. A paper that tries to *convince* is . . .

Vocabulary

Being able to define a word when you see it by itself is not as important as discovering what the word means from the clues provided by the rest of the sentence. The vocabulary words are given here in sentences similar to or the same as those used in the chapter. Select the meaning that fits the context best.

1. But the company demands to know why the *pier* fell down.
   (a) a high tower
   (b) a support for bridges
   (c) a friend equal to you in age and social position
   (d) a rope bridge _____

2. Most teachers would rather read another book than summarize what their *colleagues* said at the conference.
   (a) lawyers
   (b) school administrators
   (c) co-workers
   (d) enemies _____

3. The owner of the smashed Volkswagen hopes to avoid having his driver's license *revoked.*
   (a) taken away
   (b) renewed
   (c) made official
   (d) recorded in a public place _____

4. He won't be sent to the conference next year unless he can make his story very funny and very *relevant.*
   (a) a big surprise
   (b) complete and informative
   (c) logically connected with the problem being discussed
   (d) somewhat disrespectful and in questionable taste _____

5. He has an *urgent* need to loosen the family purse strings.
   (a) pressing
   (b) itching
   (c) temporary
   (d) peculiar _____

6. Let's look at a few purposes that make people abandon their natural *sluggishness*.
   (a) eagerness to fight
   (b) quickness of mind
   (c) slowness in getting started
   (d) bad temper and ill will   _____

7. Rats, mice, and rabbits belong to the *rodent* family.
   (a) characterized by reddish-brown hair
   (b) gnawing mammals
   (c) animals with sharp ears
   (d) the same family as cats   _____

8. Many *elementary* texts, in science or in English, for instance, are made up of explanation.
   (a) simple and easy to understand
   (b) confused and twisting
   (c) designed for grade school
   (d) highly sophisticated and technical   _____

9. The accident report must contain no analysis of the *unrestrained* nature of the other driver's driving habits.
   (a) cautious
   (b) sane
   (c) uncontrolled
   (d) unusual   _____

10. The City Council passed a zoning *ordinance* last night.
    (a) request that policemen supervising zones be armed
    (b) a rule that applies only over the weekend
    (c) a local rule
    (d) an order to the mayor to write a law   _____

11. Newspapers do not tell you the council members are a pack of *reactionary* idiots.
    (a) one whose politics you agree with
    (b) one whose political attitudes are out of date
    (c) one whose political attitudes are too liberal
    (d) one who favors violent overthrow of the government _____

12. You may find these lectures and pleas and opinions on the *editorial* page.
    (a) a straight report of the news

(b) an advertisement section
(c) the front of the paper
(d) an acknowledged expression of opinion _____

13. You may find these lectures and pleas and opinions in a *syndicated* column.
(a) always written locally
(b) published the same day in several different newspapers across the country
(c) unsuitable to print because it is often obscene
(d) published first in one newspaper and then reprinted by another without permission _____

14. Seaweed is *nutritious* and economical.
(a) inexpensive
(b) good for you
(c) entirely lacking in vitamins
(d) unattractive _____

15. "You, too, can enjoy a seaweed *soufflé*." (A suitable answer is:)
(a) "No, thank you, I'm allergic to eggs."
(b) "Yes, please, I love chocolate and pecans."
(c) "I'd rather not; I don't understand foreign plays."
(d) "No, I have to wear a back brace." _____

16. A good blend is not a *hodgepodge*.
(a) a homogeneous mixture
(b) a mammal that burrows underground
(c) a jumbled, confusing mixture
(d) a writing of single purpose _____

17. Your main idea sentence must not contain obvious *evasions*.
(a) erasures and changes
(b) avoidance of the real issue
(c) big words
(d) unskillful blending of purposes _____

18. If you begin to write without a clear main idea sentence, you will find yourself *floundering*.
(a) giving up and going fishing
(b) acting without purpose or direction
(c) discovering your real purpose as you write
(d) getting sleepier and sleepier _____

Comprehension

Answer this multiple choice quiz according to what is said in the chapter, whether or not it agrees with your own opinion. Sometimes there is more than one right answer; if so, use the letters for *all* the right answers. Sometimes there will be *no* right answer; if so, write "none" in the blank provided.

1. Any piece of writing is most likely to be effective if
   (a) the writer concentrates on getting the spelling right
   (b) the paper is neat and attractive
   (c) the writer knows clearly what the purpose of the writing is
   (d) the writer keeps that purpose in mind all the time he is writing
   (e) the writer finds the writing fun

   _____

2. The main writing purposes are
   (a) writing letters
   (b) explaining
   (c) entertaining readers
   (d) giving directions
   (e) convincing other people
   (f) doing English themes
   (g) telling what happened
   (h) discussing what happened
   (i) summarizing

   _____

3. Giving directions differs from explaining because
   (a) in giving directions the writer defines or compares or classifies or analyzes
   (b) in explanations the writer defines or compares or classifies or analyzes
   (c) in giving directions the writer talks to the reader as though he were giving commands
   (d) in giving explanations the writer talks to the reader as though he were giving commands
   (e) in explanations the writer is trying to convince the reader to change his mind about something

   _____

4. Which of the following pieces of writing has "telling what happened" as the main purpose?
   (a) a student paper analyzing the causes of ghetto unrest
   (b) a letter to a senator urging that the anti-poverty bill be passed
   (c) a newspaper article saying that Congress passed an anti-poverty bill
   (d) a condensed version of the bill that Congress passed
   (e) a story of a shooting and a rape in the elevator of the 23rd and Lilac Street Community Center

5. Probably the commonest writing purpose is
   (a) telling other people what to do
   (b) trying to get others to agree with you
   (c) comparing one thing with another
   (d) analyzing the causes of something that happened
   (e) telling what happened

6. Summarizing means
   (a) copying what someone else has written
   (b) using what someone else has said to back up your own argument
   (c) shortening what someone else has said·without changing its meaning
   (d) arguing against what someone else has said
   (e) analyzing and commenting on what someone else has said

7. Writing purposes
   (a) should never be blended
   (b) are often blended by experienced writers
   (c) can best be blended by writers who are skillful in using each method separately
   (d) should be blended one or two at a time
   (e) should each be given exactly the same emphasis if two or more are used in the same piece of writing

8. Before you write a paper on any topic, you should
   (a) choose a subject you know something about
   (b) choose a topic that will appeal to your teacher
   (c) narrow the topic down to manageable size
   (d) as soon as you have narrowed your topic, begin writing
   (e) write out a clear main idea sentence

   _____

9. A good main idea sentence
   (a) often begins with "My paper will be about . . ."
   (b) cannot be distinguished from a narrowed topic
   (c) should include everything there is to say about the topic
   (d) sometimes keeps the reader guessing as to the point the paper will make
   (e) is illustrated by, "When I was on the basketball team at Victory High."

   _____

10. A good main idea sentence
    (a) makes a clear definite statement
    (b) makes clear what the purpose of the paper will be
    (c) ought to be written after you have outlined what you are going to say
    (d) leaves the writer free to shift purposes as he wishes
    (e) is seldom useful in planning a paper

    _____

II

Giving Directions

So far this book has been telling you what to do. Now you get a chance to give some directions of your own. If you've never written any directions, you may think it's easier and more fun to tell someone else how to dig a ditch or scrub a floor than it is to do the digging or scrubbing yourself. But giving directions is not easy unless you understand two things: how to do whatever it is and how to get that knowledge down on paper clearly enough so that your reader can follow your directions.

Choosing a Topic

If you are asked to select your own topic, choose something you already know how to do. If you have never seen the insides of a stereo amplifier, you would be foolish to try to tell someone else how to build one. Or, if you have just enrolled in bowling for beginners, you are probably not expert enough to write a paper on how to avoid throwing a gutter ball. If you try to write such a paper, you can do nothing but repeat your bowling instructor's directions. He's the expert; let him write the paper.

If you suspect that the things you know how to do best would be either too obvious or too complicated, you can usually find some better topic by thinking awhile. If the topic, "how to change a tire," seems too obvious and "how to program a computer" too complicated, look for some middle ground, something personal. "How to cut a younger brother's hair" is better than either tire-changing or computer programming, but "how to keep a youngster still during a haircut" is better yet. You'll have more fun writing a set of directions that demands original thought, and your teacher will find your paper a welcome relief from paper after paper on tire-changing, cake-baking, skirt-hemming.

Main Idea Sentences for Papers Giving Directions

After you have picked your topic, but before you begin to write, work out a main idea sentence. For a paper giving directions, the main idea sentence must include two things:

1. what the directions will cover
2. the most important thing the reader needs to have or do in order to follow the directions successfully.

For instance, you might say, "The important thing to remember when you deliver a baby is to see that everything to be used is sterile." Such a sentence would make a useful main idea if you are a neighborhood midwife. If you are giving directions on something that requires less specialized knowledge, you still need to say what you are giving directions for and what the reader needs to have or do.

You can't make an extension cord without the proper tools.

(Notice that this main idea sentence tells what the job is—making an extension cord—and what is needed—the proper tools.)

Almost anybody can make rich, creamy fudge if he's careful to measure the ingredients exactly.

(This main idea sentence tells what the job is—making fudge—and the main thing to watch out for—using exact measurements.)

Although it is true that there are many ways to skin a cat, the best way is to kill it first.

(Here the reader is told what the job is and what he should do before he begins the actual job.)

Exercise 1.   Write a main idea sentence for a paper giving directions for each of the following:

1. How to make a bed.

_____

_____

_____

2. How to make a kite.

_____

_____

_____

3. How to remove a spot without leaving a stain.

_____

_____

_____

4. How to iron a shirt.

_____

_____

_____

5. How to wallpaper a small room.

_____

_____

_____

6. How to make party sandwiches.

_____

_____

_____

7. How to find a library book by using the card catalog.

_____

_____

_____

8. How to open a charge account.

_____

_____

_____

9. How to make a _____. (Fill in the blank with something you know how to make.)

_____

_____

_____

10. How to _____. (Fill in the blank with something you know how to do.)

_____

_____

_____

Planning the Paper

Working out the main idea sentence is the first step; planning the paper is the second. Beneath your main idea sentence, list all the steps needed to do the job. Check to see that you have not omitted any necessary step. Because you are dealing with a subject you are very familiar with, it is easy to leave out something that seems obvious to you. Just remember that it may not be so obvious to the reader. If you are giving directions for making fudge, don't jump from mixing the sugar and milk to stirring the mixture when it reaches the soft-ball stage. Your reader may not realize that fudge has to be cooked, or, even if he does know enough to put the pot on the stove, he may not know whether to use high, low, or medium heat, and whether to expect the soft-ball stage in five minutes or two hours. It's your job to see that he has all the information he needs, and that he has it in the right order.

For the topic, "how to start a car," your main idea sentence might be:

> If your car won't start because the motor is cold, there are a few easy things you can do that should help.

A list of the steps in the paper might be:

1. pull out choke
2. step on clutch
3. take car out of gear
4. if no start, turn off
5. step on accelerator and hold down
6. with accelerator down, turn ignition on again
7. car starts

Have any necessary steps been left out? Apparently one step is missing. The list doesn't tell us to turn the ignition on, although step 6 says to turn it on *again*. Even though the writer may think that everybody knows a car won't start without the ignition, the step must be included. Further, does the reader depress the clutch when he turns the ignition on again (step 6)? The writer knows, but the reader doesn't.

Are the steps in the right order? If "turn the ignition on" is put in just before step 4, and "depress the clutch again" before step 6, the order looks all right. Probably the order of steps 1, 2, and 3 doesn't matter much; these are all things that must be done before the "new" step 4, turning on the ignition. If you arrange all the steps in sequence, when you begin to write your paper you will be spared the agony of wondering what you should say first and what you should say next. The groundwork will be done.

Exercise 2.   Here are plans for five different papers giving directions. The steps the writer plans to cover are there, but they are listed
haphazardly. On a separate page, list them in the order that seems to you
most sensible.

1. *How to dye a pair of shoes*

   Use smooth strokes
   Pick the color you want
   Don't drip dye on clothes or furniture
   Cover the whole surface
   Be sure leather is clean
   Let shoes dry to see whether second coat is needed
   Use a clean applicator
   Be sure to get dye, not polish
   If second coat is needed, follow the same procedure

2. *How to roll a sleeping bag*

   Begin to roll from the foot of the bag
   Fold straightened bag in half lengthwise
   Straighten the bag out full length on the ground
   Tie the strings with a square knot
   Keep the roll small by squeezing it down all the time you're rolling it
   Wrap the weather flap around the rolled-up bag
   Brush off leaves, dirt, sticks, as you roll

3. *How to mat a picture*

   Buy matting paper at least a foot longer and a foot wider than the
      picture
   Use a very sharp razor
   Mark a rectangle in the center of the matting paper
   Measure the size of the picture
   You should have a metal straight edge at least as long as the biggest
      dimension of the picture
   The rectangle in the center should be a half-inch smaller on all sides
      than the picture
   You need a tape measure and some liquid adhesive
   Measure to make sure that both sides of the matting paper are exactly
      equal
   Don't hang the matted picture until it has stayed flat on the floor for
      at least twenty-four hours

Check to make sure the top and bottom of the matting are exactly
   equal
Apply a light coating of adhesive to the matting a half inch outside
   the rectangle you have cut
Make all your lines on the back of the matting paper
Gently press the picture into position, making sure it overlaps the
   matting exactly a half inch in all directions
Using the straight edge, cut the matting paper firmly along the lines
   you have drawn

4. *How to ride standby on an airplane*

If you miss the first flight, keep waiting
Present your youth ticket when you purchase your half-fare ticket
Get your standby number as soon as you've purchased your ticket
Buy a youth fare identification card if you don't already have one
Don't try to travel at the busiest hours
You will need something to show that you are between twelve and
   twenty-two
About twenty minutes before flight time, stay close to the boarding
   area so you can hear your number if it is called
Check your bags when you buy your ticket
Be sure to get to the airport an hour or two before plane time
Try for a through flight so you won't be bumped by a full-fare pas-
   senger at some intermediate airport
Take something to read while you're waiting

5. *How to fell a tree*

Using the axe, cut a notch on side of tree facing the direction you want
   tree to fall
You will need an axe, a crosscut saw, and a wedge
When tree begins to lean, yell "Timber" and get out of the way
Holding the saw horizontally, begin sawing on the side of the tree
   opposite the notch
The notch should be about two inches high and four inches deep
If crosscut begins to pinch, hammer wedge into the cut with back of
   the axe
Don't saw all the way through
Make sure the area where tree will fall is free of anything that can be
   damaged
Use axe to lop branches from the fallen tree

Writing the Introduction

Like any other essay, a paper of directions needs an introduction. How long should it be? For short papers of 200 to 500 words, the length you will usually write, a paragraph is enough. The length of the introduction is relative to the length of the writing. A ten-page essay may have as much as a page of introduction, and a book may have a whole chapter.

The purpose of an introduction is to tell the reader what the writing is going to be about and to give him a chance to decide whether to continue reading. The introduction becomes a contract between the writer and the reader. You must not go beyond what your introduction agrees to do, nor may you do less than it promises. If the main idea sentence in your first paragraph promises to tell how to deliver a baby, then your paper must be strictly limited to the problem of delivering babies. You must not drop the baby and begin telling your reader why you are against birth control. Neither can you simply take care of the sterilizing technique and leave the baby to shift for himself; somebody has to slap him to get his breathing started.

A good introduction must contain more than just a main idea sentence. It may give reasons for doing the job, it may offer encouragement, it may list the necessary equipment, it may justify the need for the first step, or it may simply arouse the reader's interest. The first paragraph certainly should include all the information the reader needs before he can start the job.

These samples show three ways of introducing a paper giving directions. In each one, the main idea sentence is italicized.

(1) If you need an extension cord but feel that ready-made ones are too expensive and usually the wrong length, you may want to try your hand at making your own. *You can't make an extension cord without the proper tools.* However, since all you need is a screwdriver, a knife, and a pair of pliers, you probably have everything you need already.

(2) Drugstores sell dozens of different candy bars and supermarkets stock hundreds, but you seldom find packaged fudge. One reason is that fudge is best when it's fresh, and it gets stale within a day or two. Another reason is that fudge is easy to make at home. If you're thinking right now that you'd like some fudge, don't settle for a candy bar. The directions are simple. *Almost anybody can make rich, creamy fudge if he's careful to measure the ingredients exactly.*

(3) *Although it is true that there are many ways to skin a cat, the best way is to kill it first.* The truth of the matter is that cats simply

don't like to be skinned, and they're downright disagreeable in revealing this prejudice. Consequently, a cat doesn't care a hang how much thought you've put into the job or how tenderly you begin. If he's alive enough to notice what you're up to, he'll be swift and terrible in his protest.

Notice that there is no single best place for the main idea sentence. It can come at the beginning, in the middle, or at the end. Notice, too, that there is no single best way to develop an introduction. Paragraph 1 gives reasons for doing the job and lists the necessary equipment. Paragraph 2 arouses the reader's interest and encourages him by saying how easy it is. Paragraph 3 justifies the need for the first step. Although all of them contain more than the bare statement of the main idea sentence, the contract they make with the reader is perfectly plain.

Exercise 3.   Be prepared to explain in class whether or not these introductory paragraphs are satisfactory for papers giving directions. If you think they are unsatisfactory, be definite about what is wrong with them.

If your teacher asks you to, rewrite each unsatisfactory introduction on a separate sheet of paper.

1. This paper is about models. I don't approve of plastic models, although many people are using them these days. The first thing is to buy a kit.

2. Get a welding torch and sheet metal ready. Clear a space in the shop. Don't forget a wrench. And don't forget some wire. Make sure you have enough room.

3. I spent last summer working as a reporter on a newspaper. They were publishing a weekly. If you want to publish a newspaper, get a printing press, some paper, and some people who will work for you. You ought to sell some advertisements.

4. After you have scrambled your eggs, serve them. To be sure they are served hot, heat the plates first.

5. This job doesn't take very long, and it isn't very hard, so that's a good thing. It also doesn't take up much room. Collect everything together, but don't forget the main piece of equipment. Once you have everything you need, you are ready to begin.

6. The first thing to do is to write a first draft and put it away for a day or two. Before that you should narrow the topic. Narrowing the topic is very important, but careful revising is a very good way to make sure you've done the best job you could on your paper.

7. To change a diaper, you need several things: a clean diaper, a can of talcum powder, two safety pins, and a dirty baby.

8. There are four kinds of students in this school. The serious student is usually found in the library. The social student can be found carrying books, but usually he's having coffee with his friends instead of reading them. The athlete wears a sweatshirt stenciled "Property of the Physical Education Department." The husband-hunter wears exotic hair-dos and lots of eye make-up.

Writing the Main Part of the Paper

Writing the main part of a paper of directions should be fairly easy; all you need do is follow your plan. But just as the main idea sentence is not enough for the first paragraph, so simply repeating the list of steps is not enough for the main part of the paper. You must do more than just copy the list you have already made. The student who made the plan on p. 31 won't have much of a paper if he writes:

> First, pull out the choke, then step on the clutch, then take the car out of gear, then turn on the ignition. If it doesn't start, turn the ignition off. Then step on the accelerator and hold it down. Depress the clutch again. With the accelerator down, turn the ignition on again. The car ought to start.

To see how this list can be expanded into a 250-word paper, examine the sample theme on p. 53. Notice that this paper makes some useful additional comment about almost every item on the list. The writer has done more than just copy his plan.

Writing the Conclusion

Just as every paper needs an introduction, so every paper must have a conclusion. The final paragraph of a paper of directions need not be very long, but it ought to give the reader the feeling that he has come to the end, not that you got tired in the middle and just stopped. The conclusion to a short paper may contain only one sentence:

(1) By making your own extension cord, you have saved some money, had the satisfaction of doing the job, and produced a cord of exactly the length you needed.

(2) Fudge made according to these directions has never been known to fail.

(3) If it turns out that cats do have nine lives, you may have to repeat this process eight more times, but at least by then you'll be an expert.

Single-sentence conclusions such as these do very well for papers of simple directions. Longer, more complicated papers need longer conclusions. But whether the conclusion to a thousand-word paper of explanation uses three paragraphs to summarize the main divisions of the paper, or whether a book defending a point of view includes a whole chapter intended to clinch the argument, all good conclusions have one thing in common: they make the writing sound finished.

Exercise 4.   Be prepared to explain in class whether or not these conclusions are satisfactory for a paper on how to build a patio. If you find them unsatisfactory, be definite about what is wrong with them.

1. When you finish smoothing the cement with the hand trowel, your patio is finished.

2. If you've followed these directions carefully, you should now have a patio that is both decorative and functional.

3. When you have finished, your knees will ache and your shoulders will be stiff, but you will have a patio that is the envy of the neighborhood.

4. When you have got the cement as smooth as you can get it, let it dry for several days before you put the furniture on it or else you will wreck your new patio before you've had it any time at all.

5. After you've finished working on the patio, clean up your tools and put them away. A neat toolshed is the mark of a good workman.

6. I have just told you how to pour the cement. Now I will tell you how to get the surface smooth. Use a hand trowel and work carefully. Be careful not to leave handprints in the soft cement.

7. Now your patio is yours to enjoy from this day forth, for better or for worse. I hope it's for better, and I hope I haven't left out any of the steps.

8. In time all things turn to dust, but if you've followed these directions carefully, your new patio should be good for at least fifty years.

9. Ashes to ashes,
   Slop to slop,
   If your cement dries too fast,
   Your patio's a flop.

10. That's all, folks.

Checking for Clarity

Just because you have written the conclusion, however, don't think your work is over. The hardest part is over, to be sure, but you still need to do the careful detective work that will improve your writing. Read through what you have written. Is everything you have said perfectly clear? Clarity is important in any kind of writing, but it is essential in giving directions.

Short sentences are more likely to make for clarity than long, involved ones. The statement "Go two blocks south and one block west" is much simpler and clearer than:

> Although I'm not absolutely sure just how you get there, I think if you go south past Hawmeyer's drugstore—that's the one with the green front across from the bank—and then on past that to the first stop light you see, and then turn up the hill—no, the hill comes a block later but you can see it from the corner—and then turn left— no, right—and turn back to the grocery store, the one with the hole in the window where the woman got shot last summer—and go about a block farther, you ought to see it right across from the city park.

"Go two blocks south and one block west" is not only clearer, it is more likely to inspire confidence.

Avoiding Apologies

Extra, unnecessary information may make your reader wonder whether you really know what you're talking about, but a continuous stream of apologies will make him sure you do not. Nothing weakens writing like apologies.

Whenever you are tempted to say, "Although I'm not sure, but I think . . ." you have only two choices: don't say it at all, or look it up and be sure. There is rarely a good reason for saying "It seems to me" or "in my opinion." Your reader can figure out that if it didn't seem that way to you, you wouldn't be saying it. And the phrase "in my opinion" usually doesn't refer to "opinion" at all. It's either a feeble attempt to make a paper longer or a confession of inadequacy. It's true that you may not be an expert on very many complicated subjects, but if you have chosen a topic you do know something about, you're probably at least as much of an expert as your reader is. Don't write on topics that will force you to apologize.

Exercise 5.   Rewrite these sentences to get rid of apologies and wordiness. If the sentences are all right as they stand, write OK.

1. It's not very hard, in my opinion, to get from Finkelmeyer's Department Store to the Hampton Overhead Bridge if you go two blocks east, turn left three blocks, and—I think—go right one or two more blocks, or maybe three.

_____

_____

_____

2. The store is on the left side of the street, about twenty feet from the corner.

_____

_____

3. It is my belief that the next step is to screw the brackets firmly in place.

_____

_____

4. The march will begin on the courthouse steps on Saturday at exactly two o'clock.

_____

_____

5. Although I'm not an expert in this subject, I'll do my best to tell you how to install a lightning rod, which, I think, shouldn't be too hard if I can explain it clearly.

_____

_____

6. The closest record store is down past the second red light, and don't forget to come to a complete stop, and then half a mile west, and you'll maybe want to look at the sports cars in a lot about half way there.

_____

_____

_____

7. After you've put the garlic into the spaghetti sauce, you should, it seems to me, taste it, or anyway I would.

_____

_____

8. In most circumstances, when it is very cloudy, I think it is likely that it might be going to rain.

_____

_____

9. To hang a picture straight, first drive the nail where you want it— no, it's better to measure it first, I think, and then drive the nail.

_____

_____

10. I'd like to tell you how to apply linoleum paste to a splintered wooden floor.

_____

_____

Using Transitions

Another way to write clearly is to take your reader with you as you move from one step to the next. Sometimes this transition from step to step occurs almost automatically. It is natural to number the steps by saying, "First, mix the chocolate and the sugar," and "Second, stir in the milk." Other words and phrases can help to suggest order:

You begin by . . .	Then . . .	The last step is to . . .
Next . . .	After you have . . .	Finally . . .

These transitional words and phrases make for smoother, easier reading, but overusing any one of them becomes tiresome: "*Then* you do this *and then* you add this *and then* you do that *and then* . . ."

Transitions that show how things are related in time are common in papers of directions, and they are sometimes used in other kinds of writing, too. Papers of explanation, however, often need transitions showing how things are related in space (*next to, beyond, in front of,* etc.) or how things contrast in our minds (*however, nevertheless, but, in spite of,* etc.). We might call these connectors *link transitions*. Usually they are single words or groups of words that we think of as one.

But sometimes we need transitions that show the logical relationship between one set of ideas and another, and we cannot find a ready-made link transition that will do the job. The best way to show this kind of logical relationship is to pick up an important word or phrase at the end of one paragraph and repeat it at the beginning of the next paragraph. For example, in this chapter we ended one paragraph by saying, ". . . all good *conclusions* have one thing in common: they make the paper sound finished," and we began the next paragraph with "Just because you have written the *conclusion,* however, . . ." We might call this kind of device an *echo transition*.

Some care must be exercised in using echo transitions smoothly. Beginning writers sometimes say, "Now I have told you how to scrape the *wires* and the next thing I am going to tell you is how to connect the *wires*." Although such phrasing does repeat what was already said, it is flatfooted and awkward because it also tells the reader that he has been told. If the reader doesn't already know that he has been told how to scrape the wires, there is something wrong with the directions; if he does know, then he doesn't need to be told again. Strike out the parts that say "I have just told you, . . . now I'm going to tell you, . . ." and instead say, "After you have scraped the wires, you should . . ." Both link and echo transitions are useful, but they should sound easy and natural. Lead your reader by the hand; don't pull him by the nose.

Exercise 6. Provide transitions so that these choppy sentences will fit together smoothly. You may combine and rearrange the sentences if you want to. Try to use words other than "then" and "and."

1. I went to hang the picture. I was nervous about it. I drove a nail in and broke out a big chunk of plaster. I started to drive another nail. I was more nervous than I was before. I hit my thumb with the hammer. I swore. I threw the hammer against the wall. The hammer knocked out some more plaster. I quit.

_____

_____

_____

_____

_____

_____

2. To hang a picture you need a hammer, a nail, and some tape. Decide where you want the picture. Figure out where the nail will have to go. Put a strip of tape on the wall where the nail will go. Pound the nail through the tape and into the wall. Leave enough nail sticking out to catch the picture wire. Hang the picture on the nail.

_____

_____

_____

_____

_____

_____

3. Starting a campfire without matches is easy. You can use a pair of glasses as a magnifying glass. The sun must be out to shine through the glasses. Collect plenty of paper, twigs, branches, and logs. The paper must be dry. Dry leaves can be substituted for paper. The twigs should be shaved very fine. Hold the glasses so that the sun shines on the paper or the leaves. Put on the small twigs after the paper or leaves catch fire. When the small twigs are burning well, add the larger branches. Put on the logs.

_____

_____

_____

_____

_____

_____

4. To change film in a box camera, follow these seven steps. Work in a fairly dark place. Turn the knob until none of the old film can be seen in the window opening. Remove the exposed film and wrap it in the foil that you have taken off the new roll. Switch the spindle to the other side. Insert the new film. Be careful not to expose any of it. Turn the new film until the first picture can be seen in the window opening. Make sure the back is tightly in place. You are ready to take pictures.

_____

_____

_____

_____

_____

_____

Keeping the Same Attitude Toward the Reader: Pronouns

You must not only lead the reader from paragraph to paragraph, you must take care of him within the paragraph, too. One way of doing that is always speaking to your reader in the same way. If you begin by speaking directly to him, keep on speaking directly to him throughout the rest of your paper. "Before one can change their tire, you must stop our car" is almost frightening. Is *our* car trying to run over *their* tire, and are *you* chasing behind trying to grab the bumper before *one* is smashed to a bloody pulp? If you mean to say, "Stop the car before you change the tire," then say so. In papers giving directions, address your reader as though you were speaking to him face to face. Say "you," "your," or simply, "do this," "don't do that." When you tell what happened to you, say, "I," "me," "we," "us." In writing about yourself it is natural to say, "I found," "we tried," "it surprised me." Feeling natural will make your writing sound natural.

Some handbooks will tell you, however, that less personal writing purposes—explanations, factual writing, papers intended to convince—should avoid both *I* and *you* and instead use more impersonal expressions such as *people, others, students, anybody.* It is true that avoiding *I, me,* and *you* will make your writing sound more formal. But if you are more comfortable speaking directly to your reader, by all means do so. Feeling comfortable may very well help you to write more clearly.

Trying to write impersonally is sometimes a strain, especially at first when you are struggling with what you want to say. In trying to write impersonally, some writers say "one should," "one tends," but *one tends* to become annoyed by this habit, *doesn't one?* Saying *one* when you mean *people* is an affectation that can easily be avoided. Whenever there is a choice between sounding affected and sounding natural, by all means be natural. Such a sentence as "One should not stay in the bathtub for more than four hours at a time" inspires the flippant reader to say, "OK, but should two do it?"

However, the way you address the reader—whether you say *I, you, he,* or *people*—is not as important as being consistent. Don't confuse your reader by skipping haphazardly from one pronoun to another in a single paper.

Making Clear What Pronouns Stand For

Readers will also be confused if they cannot tell which of two things a pronoun stands for. If you say, "Rupert told Claude *he* had made a mistake," your reader cannot tell who made the mistake. Sometimes the situation gets even more confusing: "When the people left their cars, the parking lot attendants cleaned *them*." What got cleaned, the people or the cars? "Tansy missed the premiere, *which* caused many raised eyebrows." Why were the eyebrows raised? Were Tansy's friends astonished that she didn't turn up after she had paid for her ticket? Or had the actors in the first scene taken off too many clothes?

Sometimes the reader is confused because the writer uses pronouns that don't stand for anything he has said: "I'm majoring in education, but I don't know whether I'll ever be *one*." If the writer keeps on at that rate, the chances are good that he will not become a teacher—or was becoming a teacher what he meant? Such sentences are bad, not because they are "wrong," but because they are confusing. Your job is to make whatever you are saying perfectly clear.

Exercise 7.   Rewrite these sentences to avoid any pronoun confusion.

1. Compare a Martin with a Gibson. It's a much better guitar.

_____

_____

2. Dan Gurney often talked about Bruce McLaren. He was a good driver,
   he thought, and a fierce competitor.

_____

_____

_____

3. Sally told Barbara about her mistake.

_____

_____

4. Take the lid off the paint can. Then you stir slowly but thoroughly.
   We should be sure to mix up the heavy paint at the bottom of the
   can. This will give the paint a smooth texture. When one notices that
   the thin streak of turpentine has disappeared, they know that the paint
   is ready and you are ready to begin.

_____

_____

_____

_____

_____

5. A person should pay their taxes if you don't want trouble with the government.

_____

_____

6. I've worked at a hospital and read books about nursing, but I'm not sure I'd want to be one.

_____

_____

7. Conductors know musicians so well they sometimes call them by their first names.

_____

_____

8. If one gets hit on the head with a baseball, you should lie down and rest awhile.

_____

_____

9. The title of the play was so funny that it was a help in remembering it.

_____

_____

10. Most of my friends are majoring in history but I'm not sure that I want to be one.

_____

_____

11. To sell benefit tickets, wait until the people are all seated and then charge a dollar for them.

_____

_____

12. Voters should be well informed before they cast his or her ballots.

_____

_____

13. Have the patients get out of the beds and then put clean sheets on them.

_____

_____

14. Everyone should know their emergency fire alarm number, especially if you live in a wooden house.

_____

_____

_____

15. The policeman in our block is not very polite to college kids, but you never see them hollering at doctors, especially if you make twenty thousand a year.

_____

_____

_____

_____

16. One should always carry one's draft card on one, especially if one is likely to be stopped by the police.

_____

_____

_____

17. To wash windows thoroughly, take the curtains down and spray window cleaner on them.

_____

_____

_____

18. LSD is a very hazardous thing to play with. If you take it just once, many people get recurring visions.

_____

_____

_____

19. The Diggers used to give food and clothes to anybody who came, and you weren't charged anything for it.

_____

_____

_____

20. Marta told her father that she was going to marry her boy friend if he had no objection.

_____

_____

Finding a Title

After you have written your paper and revised it as carefully as you can, the last step is to give it a title. Sometimes the simplest titles are the best. In a paper of directions, a phrase that shows clearly what the directions will cover is more effective than an attempt to be cute. "Making Your Own Extension Cord" is a better title than "To Shock or Not to Shock"; "How to Make Creamy Fudge" is better than "Sweets to the Sweet."

If you can think of a title that is both clever and clear, fine, but generally it is better not to parody a quotation so familiar that it has already been overworked (To Shock or Not to Shock), and it is always better to avoid clichés, phrases that once were bright and clever but that are now worn out by overuse (Sweets to the Sweet). Both these titles are bad because they are corny. But they are also misleading, and that is a more serious fault. The titles don't clearly indicate what the paper will be about. Because paint manufacturers don't want to mislead their customers, paint cans are usually labeled "Directions for Mixing," not "I Wish I Could Shimmy Like Enamel Can." For the same reason, the directions for assembling a chair are never headed, "Fun and Games with a Screwy Screwdriver."

You should worry more about whether your title is direct and appropriate than about whether it is dull. If you make it informative, your reader won't be bored. And sometimes you can find a fresh way to twist a phrase and still keep it appropriate. The student theme below, for instance, repeats the *m*'s in a somewhat unusual, but still quite accurate, phrase.

Avoid titles that are either too short or too long. Very short titles are likely to include too much. "Extension Cords" sounds like an encyclopedia entry, not a paper on making your own; "Creamy Fudge" sounds like a box label. Very long titles are just as unsatisfactory; good titles are seldom a whole sentence long. Your main idea sentence belongs in your first paragraph, not at the top of your paper.

When you find a title that pleases you, center it at the top of the first page. Capitalize the important words, but don't use quotation marks and don't underline. Skip a line between the title and the first paragraph, just as in the theme shown below.

And remember that the title of a theme is part of the wrapping of the package, not part of the contents. If your title is "Making Your Own Extension Cord," don't begin your first sentence by saying, "If you need a new *one* . . ." An easy way around this temptation is to write your theme *before* you give it a title, not after.

Exercise 8.   Be prepared to explain in class whether or not these titles are satisfactory for a paper on how to build a patio. If you find them unsatisfactory, be definite about what is wrong with them.

1. How to Pat a Patio

2. Making your own patio

3. Do it yourself and SAVE!

4. "A Barbecue Fad Needs A Cement Pad"

5. "How to Make Your Own Patio"

6. It's easy to make your own patio if you follow these simple directions.

7. A Midsummer Night's Dream Come True

8. Say It With Cement

9. Don't Be a Stick in the Cement

10. Cement Mixer, Putty Putty

11. Three Reasons for Building Your Own Patio

12. Anyone who has time, patience, and energy can build his own patio.

13. Good Things Come in Cement Packages

14. Who Needs Professionals?

15. A Place in the Sun

16. How to Build a Patio

17. How to build a patio

18. "How to Build a Patio"

19. How to Build a Patio

20. How To Build A Patio

Examining a Sample Theme

Here is a student theme giving directions on how to start a car:

Moving the Motor

(1)   If you drive a car very often, you have probably experienced times when you just couldn't get it to start. If, as is often the case, your motor is just cold, there are a few steps you can take which should help in starting the car.

(2)   The first thing to do is to pull out the choke. (Some cars have no manual choke, and in this case, all you can do is hope that the automatic choke works.) If you have a hand choke, pull it out all the way.

(3)   Next, if you have a car with manual shifting, step on the clutch and take the car out of gear. If you drive a car with an automatic transmission, make sure it is in neutral.

(4)   After you have pulled out the choke and disengaged the gears, you are ready to turn on the ignition. Do so, and see if your car starts. If it doesn't start within a few seconds, turn off the ignition. If the engine keeps turning over without starting, it may become flooded, which only makes it worse.

(5)   Instead, after turning the key off, step on the accelerator and hold it all the way down for about ten seconds. *Don't pump it.* Pumping can also flood the engine. Still holding the throttle down, depress the clutch, and turn the ignition on again. If your car is going to start, this try should do it.

(6)   If your car starts, you are off for school; if it doesn't, call a mechanic.

Let's examine this theme just as you should examine your own before you copy it for the last time:

Does the introductory paragraph contain a main idea sentence? Yes, but it is not the first sentence. The first sentence gives reasons for the directions; the second sentence contains the main idea. The main idea sentence tells what the theme will be about (starting a car) and suggests that these directions will work only under certain conditions (if the failure to start is because the car is cold).

Now check the theme for completeness. Are any necessary steps left out? The student tells you to pull out the choke, disengage the gears, and turn on the ignition, but what about the starter? Perhaps all the cars he has driven have the starter connected with the ignition, but do all cars?

The order is all right. It follows the plan that has already been checked.

Notice that the student has avoided all namby-pamby phrases. He does not pretend to be an absolute authority, but he is writing about something he is familiar with, and his writing is straightforward and unapologetic.

Is the theme clear? The writer does address the reader as "you" all through the paper and thus avoids jumping from pronoun to pronoun. Are there any pronouns which can stand for more than one thing? In paragraph 3, the writer tells you to "make sure it is in neutral," but does *it* refer to the car or the transmission? Do we need to know whether *it* means the car or the transmission? Since the difference is not confusing, worrying about what the *it* refers to is just quibbling. The fourth paragraph, however, says that to keep the engine turning when it is not starting may cause *it* to "become flooded, which only makes *it* worse." The first *it* is the engine, but what is the second one? Can we make an engine *worse*? Or does the student mean that a flooded engine will make the *situation* worse? This pronoun confusion is more serious than the one in paragraph three. Putting a car in neutral is about the same as putting its transmission in neutral, but making a motor worse (perhaps damaging it) is quite a bit different from making the situation worse (not necessarily damaging the motor, but adding to your general frustration).

Does the student use transitions to take the reader easily from point to point? As a matter of fact, he uses the two kinds we have discussed. Paragraph 2 begins with "The first thing to do . . ."; paragraph 3 begins with "Next . . ."; and paragraph 4 begins "After you have . . ." These link transitions show the order of the steps. The transition between paragraphs 4 and 5 echoes an important idea. In paragraph 4 the writer has said ". . . turn off the ignition." He begins paragraph 5 by saying ". . . after turning the key off . . ."

Most of this theme is perfectly clear.

A Check List for Revisions

Your paper may seem clear to you at the time you write it, but if you put it away for a day or two before rereading it, you may find confusions that you missed. Reading your paper aloud to yourself also helps, and it is even better to read it to somebody else, if you can find someone who will put politeness aside long enough to tell you when you are confusing him.

Change the awkward parts you can *hear*, as well as those you can *see*, and then, before you hand the paper in, go back for one final check:

1. Have you done everything your first paragraph promised and no more?
2. Have you included all the necessary steps in logical order?

3. Have you cut out all the apologies?
4. Have you used enough transitions to take your reader comfortably from point to point?
5. Have you talked to your reader as the same person all the way through?
6. Is the meaning of each pronoun unmistakable?
7. Does your last paragraph fit with your first paragraph and make your paper sound finished?
8. Is your title clear and appropriate?

Exercise 9.   From the main idea sentences you wrote for Exercise 1, choose the three you know the most about. Using your own paper, list all the steps needed for each set of directions. Make sure the steps are in the right order.

Exercise 10.   Write introductory paragraphs for each of the papers you have planned in Exercise 9.

Exercise 11.   Write conclusions for each of the papers you have planned in Exercise 9.

Exercise 12.   Write one of the papers you planned in Exercises 9, 10, and 11. When you have finished, give it an appropriate title.

Exercise 13.   Find a magazine or newspaper article of at least eight consecutive paragraphs. Clip the article and bring it to class with the transitions underlined. In choosing your article, you should:

1. find one that uses good transitions;
2. avoid straight news stories and fiction, since neither of these makes much use of the kind of transitions we have been talking about.

Exercise 14.   A paper of directions for getting from one place to another involves a special kind of skill. Write a paper in which you do one of these things:

1. Give directions for going from the center of town to wherever you live, either by walking or by using public transportation.
2. Give directions for driving a car from one place to another place two or three miles away. Choose a route that involves at least three turns or choices.

In either of these papers, be sure to identify landmarks clearly enough that your reader will be able to follow your directions. Before you turn the paper in, ask yourself all the questions listed on p. 54.

Key Words

Here are some of the important terms used in this chapter. See whether you can answer these questions about them.

1. The *main idea sentence* of a paper giving directions ought to contain two things. What are they?

2. In a paper giving directions, what does the *introduction* do that the main idea sentence does not do? In what sense does the introduction serve as a *contract* with the reader?

3. How does the *main part* of a paper differ from the plan?

4. How does the *conclusion* of a paper differ from just stopping?

5. Describe in your own words what "clear" means when applied to themes. Is it true that *clarity* is particularly important in a paper giving directions? Why? Why not?

6. Why should you *avoid apologies*?

7. What is a *transition*? How does it contribute to clarity? Describe the two kinds of transitions.

8. How can the careful use of *pronouns* contribute to *clarity*? How can the two kinds of pronoun confusion be avoided?

9. What makes a good *title*?

10. Why and when should you *read* your paper *aloud*?

Vocabulary

The vocabulary words are given here in sentences similar to or the same as those used in the chapter. Select the meaning that fits the context best.

1. The important thing to remember when you deliver a baby is to see that everything to be used is *sterile*.
    (a) clean
    (b) modern
    (c) germ-free
    (d) barren _____

2. Such a sentence would make a useful main idea if you are a neighborhood *midwife*.
    (a) a woman about to have a baby
    (b) a woman who assists at a birth
    (c) a woman who has had several children
    (d) a licensed physician _____

3. If you arrange all the steps in *sequence*, when you begin to write your paper you will be spared the agony of wondering what you should say first and what you should say next.
    (a) alphabetical order
    (b) order in which the steps should be done
    (c) order in which you think of them
    (d) a pattern of simplest first, most complicated last _____

4. The length of the introduction is *relative* to the length of the writing.
    (a) in proportion to
    (b) out of proportion with
    (c) subordinate to
    (d) less important than _____

5. A good introduction may *justify* the need for the first step.
    (a) give a satisfactory reason for it
    (b) show that it is fair and equitable
    (c) apologize for it
    (d) tell a story about it _____

6. To see how this list can be *expanded* into a 250-word paper, examine the following sample theme.
   (a) distorted
   (b) dilated
   (c) developed
   (d) corrected _____

7. The phrase "in my opinion" is either a feeble attempt to make a paper longer or a confession of *inadequacy*.
   (a) uncertainty
   (b) inability to deal with the subject
   (c) recklessness
   (d) unwillingness to consult a recognized authority _____

8. Strike out these *namby-pamby* phrases wherever they occur.
   (a) direct and vigorous
   (b) characteristic of regional dialect
   (c) weak and pointless, adding nothing but words
   (d) naive and innocent _____

9. Use transitions that *echo* an important word or phrase.
   (a) repeat, slightly changed
   (b) shout, very loud
   (c) speak softly, whisper
   (d) eliminate _____

10. Trying to write *impersonally* is sometimes a strain.
    (a) by shifting from person to person as you write
    (b) by impersonating somebody else
    (c) by keeping the writer out of it as much as possible
    (d) by addressing the reader informally _____

11. People *tend* to become annoyed by this habit, don't they?
    (a) ought to
    (b) are inclined to
    (c) give attention to
    (d) take care of _____

12. Saying "one" when you mean "people" is an *affectation* that can easily be avoided.
    (a) error
    (b) natural tendency
    (c) a form of showing off
    (d) an unconscious slip _____

13. Such a sentence inspires the *flippant* reader to say, "OK, but should two do it?"
    (a) given to being unjustifiably critical
    (b) with a habit of reading haphazardly
    (c) tending to treat serious matters lightly
    (d) being nimble and quick   _____

14. Don't confuse your reader by skipping *haphazardly* from one pronoun to another in a single paper.
    (a) with complete good nature
    (b) entirely by chance
    (c) with considerable danger
    (d) in spite of the obstacles   _____

15. Many eyebrows were raised because Tansy missed the *premiere*.
    (a) the head of state
    (b) the opening performance
    (c) the very simple explanation
    (d) the fuse leading to the cannon   _____

16. Generally it is better not to *parody* a quotation so familiar that it has already been overworked.
    (a) use without giving credit
    (b) alter in an obvious and ridiculous manner
    (c) repeat without understanding
    (d) fail to quote correctly   _____

17. Since the difference is not confusing, worrying about what the "it" refers to is just *quibbling*.
    (a) a kind of betrayal
    (b) careless writing
    (c) a petty objection
    (d) correction of a pronoun error   _____

Comprehension

Answer this multiple choice quiz according to what is said in the chapter, whether or not it agrees with your own opinion. Sometimes there is more than one right answer; if so, use the letters for *all* the right answers. Sometimes there will be *no* right answer; if so, write "none" in the blank provided.

1. Good topics for papers giving directions should
   (a) require some original thought
   (b) be something complicated
   (c) be about something you know quite well how to do
   (d) be about something you aren't expert in but have some interest in
   (e) be about something you have just learned in class

   _____

2. A good main idea sentence for a paper of directions will tell
   (a) the source of your information
   (b) why you couldn't write a better paper
   (c) what the directions will cover
   (d) what the most important things are that the reader will need to have or do in order to follow the instructions
   (e) when the event took place

   _____

3. In making a plan for a paper of directions, you will want to
   (a) make a formal outline
   (b) ask for help
   (c) consult your dictionary
   (d) list the steps
   (e) check for completeness
   (f) check for order

   _____

4. The introduction is different from the main idea sentence because the introduction also
   (a) tells what the job will be
   (b) tells what the reader will need to have or do in order to follow the directions
   (c) offers encouragement or gives reasons for doing the job
   (d) tells when the event took place
   (e) talks about things not related at all to the main idea sentence

   _____

5. The best place for the main idea sentence in the introduction is
   (a) the first sentence
   (b) somewhere in the middle
   (c) the last sentence
   (d) first, middle, or last; there is no single best place
   (e) in all three places, for emphasis

   _____

6. The conclusion of a paper of directions should
   (a) repeat the introduction exactly
   (b) always be more than a single sentence
   (c) make the paper sound finished
   (d) be omitted
   (e) defend the writer's argument

   _____

7. Transitions
   (a) help to take the reader step by step
   (b) contribute to clarity
   (c) link one paragraph to the next
   (d) often echo an important word or phrase
   (e) should sound easy and natural

   _____

8. Pronoun confusion occurs when
   (a) the writer skips haphazardly from one pronoun to another
   (b) the reader cannot tell what the pronoun stands for
   (c) the writer says "you" instead of "one"
   (d) the writer says "one" instead of "you"
   (e) more than one pronoun is used in the sentence

   _____

9. Good titles for papers of definition
   (a) must be complex
   (b) must be clever and original
   (c) should clearly show what the directions will cover
   (d) are always underlined
   (e) capitalize the important words

   _____

10. If you read your paper aloud a day or two after you have written it,
    you may
    (a) find your voice and diction improving
    (b) be surprised at how well you read
    (c) miss the deadline on which the paper was due
    (d) discover and correct confusions you didn't see before
    (e) eliminate all pronouns and transitions

    _____

III

Explaining: Definition

Whenever someone says, "What do you mean?" he is asking for an explanation. Perhaps the simplest form of explanation is the one you get when you look up a word in a dictionary. However, many words cannot be satisfactorily explained by the three- or four-word definitions the dictionary offers. It takes three or four sentences to explain even a simple word like *chair* clearly enough to distinguish it from a *davenport* or a *bench*. You will find that it takes at least three or four paragraphs to explain words like *loyalty* or *love*. And there are words that require even more explanation. People have written entire books explaining the meaning of such terms as *democracy* and *freedom* and still haven't covered everything that could have been said.

When you are asked to write a paper of definition, you will probably be expected to deal with words like *loyalty* rather than words like *chair*. Such words as *chair, pencil, taxicab, cow,* refer to things we can see or hear or touch; usually there is not much disagreement about what a taxicab is, very little trouble about recognizing a cow. But words like *loyalty, courage, freedom, democracy,* refer to ideas that cannot be seen or heard or touched. These words refer to abstract concepts rather than physical things, and their meaning is much more slippery. For one thing, their meanings change from century to century: in Beowulf's time, *loyalty* meant sharing all your loot with your leader; now, no matter how loyal you are to your friends, no one except the government expects a slice of your salary. For another, meanings of abstract words shift from discussion to discussion, from group to group. You sometimes hear people say, "For purposes of the argument, let's agree that *democracy* means . . ." and then go on from there. Consequently, if you are asked to define a word like *loyalty* or *honesty* or *cowardice*, remember that you do not need to define it absolutely, for all time, or even in such a way that everybody will agree with you. Instead, your job is simply to make perfectly clear what the word means to you on the day you are writing the paper. If you are defining *cowardice*, you must be definite enough in your definition that anyone reading your paper will be able to say, "Well, *according to his definition*, Tom was a coward, Tim was not."

You must be definite, but you must be inclusive, too. And herein lies the problem. You certainly don't need to include everything that cowardice could possibly mean to anybody at any time, nor do you need to include all kinds of cowardice, if you think there is more than one kind. Unless your concept of cowardice is somewhat narrowed, you won't be able to deal with it in a 500-word paper. Still, you must keep it broad enough to include all the occasions on which the kind of cowardice you are talking about might be shown. If you don't ordinarily examine statements to see how inclusive they are, if you aren't used to thinking about whether words are general or specific, you may need some practice before you begin your definition paper.

General and Specific Words; Generalizations and Examples

We can explain *general* words by saying that the more things a word refers to, the more general it is. The fewer things a word refers to, the more *specific* it is. Thus *general* and *specific* are relative terms. The word *dog* is more specific than *animal*, less specific than *bulldog*. *Bulldog*, in turn, is less specific than *Tige*, Buster Brown's bulldog. In the same way, *human being* is more general than *college student*. *College student* is more general than *Raglan College freshman*. *Raglan College freshman* is more general than *Rupert Creech*. If you begin with *human being*, *Rupert Creech* is about as specific as you can get.

General and specific words are not bad or good in themselves; a word is good if it fits the circumstances, it is bad if it does not. You can't go wrong if you follow this rule:

> *Always choose the most specific word that will fit the subject you are discussing.*

The more general the words you use in making a statement, the more inclusive the statement will be; if the statement includes a group of people or things, or covers more than one situation, we call it a *generalization*. Some occasions demand generalizations. In the comment, "Students who finish the test early may leave," *students* is more general than *Rupert Creech* or *Tansy Ragwort*. The teacher who made the statement, however, meant not only Rupert and Tansy but any other student who might get through in a half hour. The teacher used a word as general as he needed, but he also kept it as specific as he could and still cover the situation. Notice that he did not say *human beings* or *mammals*, since he was not expecting test papers from other members of these more general classes.

On the other hand, if you offer your father the generalization, "Lots of people I know get a great big allowance," he is likely to respond, "What do you mean by 'great big'?" And when you have made that part of your statement more specific ("great big means a hundred dollars a week"), your father may still ask for an example: "Who, for instance?" He wants a specific statement.

A *generalization* includes many things, a *specific statement* concerns one particular thing. If the general statement and the specific statement are related, we say that *the specific statement is an example of the generalization*.

Generalization: Lots of people get a great big allowance.
Example: Peter Simpson gets a hundred dollars a week.

Notice, however, that if Peter Simpson is the only example you can think of, your generalization about "lots of people" will be pretty hard to defend. What is true for words goes for statements, too. Never make a more general statement than the occasion demands or the circumstances justify.

Exercise 1.   Number each of these groups of words in order, from the *most general* to the *most specific*.

2   1   3   4

EXAMPLE: building, shelter, school, classroom building

1. book, publication, A *Tale of Two Cities*, novel

2. food, grape, fruit, Concord

3. flats, clothing, shoes, black patent leather with bows

4. tools, equipment, wrenches, crescent wrenches

5. animal, human being, Indian, Sitting Bull

6. mammals, living things, females, Mae West

7. Protestantism, Christianity, religion, Presbyterianism

8. music, art, Beethoven's Fifth, concerto

9. bongos, drums, musical instruments, noisemakers

10. transportation, Volkswagen, automobile, four-wheeled vehicle

11. Rose Bowl game, football, contest, sport

12. furniture, wood product, stool, colonial milking stool

Exercise 2. For each of these words, find one word or phrase that is more general and one word or phrase that is more specific.

EXAMPLE:

vegetation	tree	_sycamore_
GENERAL		SPECIFIC

1. _____ orphan _____

2. _____ house _____

3. _____ child _____

4. _____ chair _____

5. _____ actress _____

6. _____ swimming _____

7. _____ people _____

8. _____ vegetable _____

9. _____ book _____

10. _____ teacher _____

11. _____ dogs _____

12. _____ textbook _____

13. _____ baby _____

14. _____ human being _____

15. _____ sewing _____

16. _____ janitor _____

17. _____ dish _____

18. _____ sport _____

Exercise 3.   For each of the following generalizations, find a specific example that illustrates it.

> GENERALIZATION: Smoking is bad for the health.
> SPECIFIC EXAMPLE: Aunt Agatha smoked a carton of cigarettes a
>   day every day of her life, and died at age fifteen.

1. Everybody who likes dogs can be trusted.

_____

_____

_____

2. Driving on ice is dangerous.

_____

_____

_____

3. Competent drivers are as safe driving in icy weather as in any other kind of weather.

_____

_____

_____

4. Music cheers people up.

_____

_____

_____

5. Children without brothers or sisters are usually spoiled.

_____

_____

_____

6. Getting your feet wet is likely to lead to pneumonia.

_____

_____

_____

7. State patrolmen are kind and considerate to motorists.

_____

_____

_____

8. State patrolmen are rude and inconsiderate.

_____

_____

_____

9. Telephones are a great help and convenience.

_____

_____

_____

10. Telephones are a nuisance.

_____

_____

_____

Exercise 4.   Write generalizations based on these specific situations.

EXAMPLE: A small Boy Scout helped an old lady across the street.
GENERALIZATION: Boy Scouts are helpful.

1. My uncle Bertram lives in a nice modern house with lots of glass in it. Last Saturday he threw rocks at the kids playing in his front yard, and last night the kids heaved a brick through Uncle Bertram's big front window.

_____

_____

2. My cat fell off the roof and broke its neck, trying to find out what was in the chimney.

_____

_____

3. Old Man Tuttle went to bed every night at 8 P.M. and got up every morning at 6:20. He died at the age of one hundred and three, when a truck ran over him. When he died, he had a million dollars in the bank.

_____

_____

4. Algernon Creech, a college graduate, died in the poorhouse.

_____

_____

5. My lot is a hundred feet long and fifty feet wide, so it must have an area of five thousand square feet.

_____

_____

Main Idea Sentences for Papers
of Definition

Whenever you are defining an abstract term, you want your definition to apply to more than one occasion; naturally your main idea sentence will be a generalization. Remember, however, that you don't want to be any more general than you have to be. As you organize your thoughts, you will probably start by putting the term you are defining into a general class. You may, for example, decide that loyalty is a kind of determination. However, "Loyalty is determination" is obviously too general, since there are many different kinds of determination that have nothing to do with loyalty: a determination to get rich, to become famous, to look out for your own interests, to get to bed early for once—in fact, as many kinds of determination as there are varieties of human motives. You need to say something more. You might say, "Loyalty is a determination *not to abandon the people you love.*" Now you have shown how loyalty differs from the other kinds of determination.

If we look at the finished statement, we can see that it has three parts: (1) the term you are defining (loyalty); (2) the general class the term belongs in (determination); and (3) the way the term differs from other terms in the general class (not to abandon the people you love). This three-part sentence is a generalization that seems just as inclusive as you need it to be, and no more.

Now that you have worked out your main idea sentence, as you write the paper you will need to back up this generalization by specific examples. The generalization gives a broad idea of what you mean; the examples will illustrate it and show specifically what you mean. Who, for instance, refused to abandon what?

Perhaps you will say, "The faithful old dog who refuses to move more than four inches from his dead master's bathrobe is showing canine loyalty." And then you remember Barbara Frietchie, so you say, "The gallant old lady who leaned out the window and cried, 'Shoot if you must this old gray head, but spare your country's flag,' is showing loyalty, too." But look again at your main idea sentence: was Barbara Frietchie being loyal to people or to her country's flag? Your main idea sentence promised to define only one kind, personal loyalty. But your second example shows that there are at least two kinds of loyalty, loyalty to people and loyalty to country. Either you will have to make your main idea sentence general enough to include both kinds (Loyalty means a determination not to abandon the people *or the country* you love) or you will have to throw out the Barbara Frietchie example and find some others that show people being loyal to people. Probably the second choice would be better; there is a limit to what you can cover in 500 words. But whichever you decide to do, remember that *the examples must fit the definition.*

If you decide to stick with people and exclude loyalty to country or loyalty to ideas, you can probably think of other examples without too much trouble. You might say, "The girl who visited her boy friend every Sunday the whole year he was in jail showed loyalty," or "Tansy stayed loyal to Rupert even though everybody in school called him stupid. Every time she heard somebody claim he hadn't brains enough to get through the third grade, she said, 'That simply isn't true. It took him three years, but he did pass, and if he had to do it over, he could pass again right now today.'"

After you have listed the clearest examples you can think of to show what loyalty is, you may want to distinguish between loyalty and some of the things that might be confused with it. "Being loyal does not mean giving up your right to say what you think. Tansy was not being disloyal to Rupert just because she told him frankly that he had a week's accumulation of spaghetti sauce on his chin, and that if he didn't clean himself up a little, no respectable person would be seen with him." In explaining what loyalty is not, you need deal only with the one or two things that might reasonably cause confusion; you couldn't possibly give examples of everything loyalty isn't, and you would be silly to try. In arranging your examples, it is probably wise to show what the term means before you show what it doesn't mean.

Remember that the assignment is to define, not to defend, not to attack. Don't come out in favor of what you are defining, and don't come out against it either. Words such as *should* or *should not, ought* or *ought not, good* or *bad, better* or *worse,* express opinion and have no place in explanations. If you have written a clear main idea sentence, you are more likely to stick to the job of defining. You will be less tempted to say, "Everybody ought to be loyal."

Exercise 5.   Write a main idea sentence for a paper of *definition* for any five of these topics. If you think any of these terms is too broad, define only one of its possible meanings. For instance, in defining *love*, you might limit yourself to the love of a child for his parents or to puppy love or brotherly love. Be sure your generalization contains all three parts discussed on p. 72.

1. treason _____

_____

_____

2. ambition _____

_____

_____

3. wealth _____

_____

_____

4. good books _____

_____

_____

5. bad books _____

_____

_____

6. knowledge _____

_____

_____

7. wisdom _____

_____

_____

8. responsibility _____

_____

_____

9. revolution _____

_____

_____

10. hippy _____

_____

_____

Paragraphing

Whatever it is you are defining, begin with a generalization and find examples that fit it. As you write your paper, you will probably need a separate paragraph for each of your examples. Remember that these separate points are somewhat like women, each with a particular charm, each worthy of undivided attention. But just as two women in the same house may bicker and bite in competing for your attention, so will two of your points clash if you dump them into the same paragraph. Keep each woman in her own house and each point in its own paragraph.

Of course there are some niceties that will help. If you can leave one point gracefully and take up the next one smoothly, you will have a pleasanter theme, just as you will have a happier life if you can move from woman to woman without jolting either one of them—that is, visit your mother and not offend your wife. In the last chapter you had some practice in transitions, especially such simple devices as saying *then, next,* and *finally,* or *nevertheless, on the other hand, also.* By now you may have discovered that smooth relations between paragraphs, like smooth relations with women, is largely a matter of experience.

When you have finished the paper, check your first paragraph to make sure that it contains your main idea; check the rest of your paper to make sure that it does what your first paragraph promised and no more; check your final paragraph to make sure that it relates clearly to the idea presented in the first paragraph. Put your paper away to cool, and when it is thoroughly cold—in a day or two—go over it to make sure that everything you have written makes sense and that your paper does make clear what you mean.

Examining a Sample Theme

Here is a student theme defining courage:

Courage

(1)   Courage is a quality which has been valued and praised in every society in every century. Courage is the ability and the desire to hold true to principles and stand up and be counted without thought of personal gain or loss.

(2)   People often consider the war hero who plunges through a wall of fire to rescue his smoldering buddy brave, but unless he was really thinking just about his good friend, Archie, he was not demonstrating true courage.

(3)   On the other hand, America's classic example of cowardice, Benedict Arnold, may have demonstrated the greatest courage if, when he sold out to the British, he did so because of his personal convictions and a belief that in becoming a traitor he was actually promoting the best good for the most people.

(4)   Courage is not always shown in big acts, either. The grimy little boy who can go up to his teacher and stammer, "Mr. Legree, I'm sorry, but I cheated on that test," is probably displaying as much courage as the White House Aide who says, "Mr. President, I'm sorry, but I lost that last dispatch." Both of these people feel strongly enough about honesty (although apparently the third grader had a bit of a struggle) to admit to their higher authorities that they have made a mistake. Often confessing to somebody else that you have done something wrong requires the highest kind of courage.

(5)   The word "courage" comes from the Latin word *cor* which means "heart." Courage, then, is an affair of the heart which requires complete devotion of the mind and the body.

Do you understand what this student means by courage? That is, has he made his meaning exact enough that you can say to yourself, "*This* kind of behavior he would call courageous, but *that* kind he would not"? Would the writer think that pulling a drowning baby out of a pond showed courage? What would he say about joining a peace march? What would he say about driving ninety miles an hour in a forty-mile zone? Parachute jumping? Refusing to take a drink even though everybody else calls you a sissy? All these kinds of behavior are sometimes called courageous; do they all fit the student's definition?

The main idea sentence of the paper is: "Courage is the ability and the desire to hold true to principles and stand up and be counted without thought of personal gain or loss." What are the three parts of this definition? The term being defined is courage, of course, but is the general class *ability and desire* or is it *ability and desire to hold true to principles and stand up and be counted*? Actually, it doesn't make much difference which you decide. If you think that *ability and desire* is the general class, then there are two steps in showing how courage differs from other abilities and desires: first, *to hold true to principles and stand up and be counted;* second, *without thought of personal gain or loss.* If you feel more comfortable dividing all your definitions into just three parts, you will come up with:

1. courage
2. is the ability and desire to hold true to principles and stand up and be counted
3. without thought of personal gain or loss.

Whichever way you decide to do it, the definition seems to rule out what is usually called "physical bravery": a willingness to risk getting hurt or killed. Apparently parachute jumping, driving at high speed, and accepting dares would not come under this definition.

The writer's intention to exclude physical courage is suggested by his example of what courage is not: rescuing a friend during battle, the writer says, doesn't count. But why it doesn't count is not made very clear. Did the war hero rescue his friend because of principles or because he wasn't afraid of the physical danger? It is impossible to decide,' since there's no way of knowing what the hero was thinking at the time.

The two examples showing what courage is are clearer than the one that explains what it is not. First, the student suggests that Benedict Arnold might have been motivated by a real belief in the British cause. Second, he says that confessing a fault is a courageous act. Both examples show people standing up for their beliefs. In other words, they show *moral courage.*

This paper is fairly good; it would be better, however, if the student said in his introduction that there are two kinds of courage, physical and moral, but that he is concerned only with moral courage. If he limits his definition to moral courage, we will be fairly safe in saying that the writer would find that joining a peace march and refusing a drink were courageous acts. The marcher believes in demonstrating for peace, the non-drinker believes in abstinence.

The last paragraph of this paper is an attempt to make the paper sound finished by restating the definition. Half of the attempt succeeds; the paper doesn't just stop in midair. But the restatement of the definition is much less successful. The final sentence sounds more like a definition of marriage than of courage. The last paragraph needs to be rewritten.

The following second draft of the same theme is certainly much better. All of the new material has been underlined so that you can see the changes easily.

Courage

(1)   Courage is a quality which has been valued and praised in every society in every century. Everybody admires people who show courage, but not everybody agrees about what courage is. Actually, there are two kinds of courage, physical courage and moral courage.

Physical courage means not being afraid to get hurt. Moral courage is the ability and the desire to hold true to principles and stand up and be counted without thought of personal gain or loss. Physical courage is easier to see than moral courage and is more likely to be praised. Because moral courage seldom gets any medals, and because it is really harder to achieve, the person who has moral courage is showing true courage.

(2)   People often consider the war hero brave. They admire a man who plunges through a wall of fire to rescue his smoldering buddy. But even though he risked his life for his good friend, Archie, he did not have to use any moral courage. Everybody believes in saving friends.

(3)   On the other hand, America's classic example of cowardice, Benedict Arnold, may have demonstrated the greatest courage if, when he sold out to the British, he did so because of his personal convictions and a belief that in becoming a traitor he was actually promoting the best good for the most people.

(4)   Courage is not always shown in big acts, either. The grimy little boy who can go up to his teacher and stammer, "Mr. Legree, I'm sorry, but I cheated on that test," is probably displaying as much courage as the White House Aide who says, "Mr. President, I'm sorry, but I lost that last dispatch." Although apparently the third grader had a bit of a struggle, both of these people feel strongly enough about honesty to admit that they have made a mistake. Often confessing to somebody else that you have done something wrong requires the highest kind of courage.

(5)   The word "courage" comes from the Latin word *cor* which means "heart." Courage, then, means that if you believe with your whole heart that something is right, you act according to your belief.

In this second draft, the student has narrowed his definition by limiting himself to moral courage, taken care of the confusion in the second paragraph, and rewritten his conclusion. In addition, he has changed two sentences to make them read a little more smoothly: one is in paragraph 2 and one in paragraph 4.

Notice that in both drafts the student has been specific whenever he could. He has given the buddy a name, so that we think of him as a person rather than as a vague "friend." He has let us see the little boy as "grimy" and told us that he "stammered" when he made his confession. He has let us hear both the child and the aide by giving us their own words rather than his indirect version of what they said. The choice of specific words not only makes the meaning clearer but also makes the paper more interesting.

Exercise 6.   Choose a topic from Exercise 5 and make plans for a paper of definition. This is not a reference project; choose a topic you already know something about. Be sure you can defend the order of each step in your plan.

Definition of: _____

Main idea sentence: _____

_____

_____

Examples of what it is:

1. _____

_____

_____

2. _____

_____

_____

3. _____

_____

_____

Example of what it is not: _____

_____

Conclusion (*use a variation of your main idea sentence here*): _____

_____

_____

Exercise 7.   On a separate sheet, write an introductory *paragraph* and a concluding *paragraph* for a paper of definition, using one of the topics you have already outlined. Base these paragraphs on the introductory and concluding sentences, as they appear in your plan. Be sure the introductory paragraph makes clear what you are going to do and that the conclusion relates to the introduction and makes the paper sound finished.

Exercise 8.   Write a theme from the plan you made for Exercises 6 and 7. Remember that you will make your examples clearer if you refer to a definite situation and use specific words. Before you hand in your theme, underline all the transitions between paragraphs.

Key Words

Here are some of the important terms used in this chapter. See whether you can answer these questions about them.

1. Explain what is meant by the statement, "*General* and *specific* are *relative* terms."

2. In your own writing, how should you decide whether to use a *general* or a *specific word*?

3. What does *generalization* mean?

4. What does *a specific statement* mean?

5. There is the same kind of relationship between *generalizations* and *examples* as there is between *general words* and *specific words*. Without quoting from the chapter, explain these relationships.

6. What three parts should a *main idea sentence* for a paper of *definition* contain?

7. Why are *abstract words* hard to define?

8. What is one easy way to decide when you need a new *paragraph*? How can you link your paragraphs together smoothly?

Vocabulary

The vocabulary words are given here in sentences similar to or the same as those used in the chapter. Select the meaning that fits the context best.

1. It takes three or four sentences to explain even a simple word like "chair" clearly enough to *distinguish* it from a "davenport" or a "bench."
   (a) make it seem more important than
   (b) make it seem more elegant than
   (c) show how it is different from
   (d) show ways in which it is alike _____

2. "Loyalty meant sharing all your *loot* with your leader."
   (a) ideas
   (b) food
   (c) trouble
   (d) booty _____

3. Meanings of *abstract* words shift from discussion to discussion.
   (a) having to do with ideas rather than physical things
   (b) having to do with the location of real estate
   (c) having to do with mathematical terms rather than emotions
   (d) having to do with the ridiculous rather than the serious _____

4. You must be definite, but you must be *inclusive*, too.
   (a) given to discriminating against some people
   (b) covering all items
   (c) omitting irrelevant items
   (d) firm-minded, certain _____

5. Unless your *concept* of cowardice is somewhat narrowed, you won't be able to deal with it in a 500-word paper.
   (a) idea of
   (b) opinion of
   (c) experience with
   (d) emotional reaction to _____

6. Notice that he did not say "human beings" or "*mammals*."
   - (a) a group in which human beings fit
   - (b) a group separate from human beings
   - (c) a group smaller than human beings
   - (d) insects
   _____

7. Your father is likely to *respond*, "What do you mean by 'great big'?"
   - (a) do research
   - (b) repeat again
   - (c) reply
   - (d) answer in anger
   _____

8. You will probably start by putting the term you are defining into a general *class*.
   - (a) a category that has several members
   - (b) a group of pupils
   - (c) a group of people of the same social status
   - (d) a category that has high prestige
   _____

9. Loyalty is a determination not to *abandon* the people you love.
   - (a) insult
   - (b) hurt
   - (c) forsake
   - (d) vilify
   _____

10. That shows *canine* loyalty.
    - (a) doglike
    - (b) to the ninth degree
    - (c) childish
    - (d) slight
    _____

11. He had a week's *accumulation* of spaghetti sauce on his chin.
    - (a) growth
    - (b) smear
    - (c) collection
    - (d) suggestion of
    _____

12. Each is *worthy* of undivided attention.
    - (a) deserving
    - (b) worried about
    - (c) not worth
    - (d) incapable
    _____

13. There are some *niceties* that will help.
    (a) good manners
    (b) pleasantries
    (c) fine points
    (d) gifts
    _____

14. The *grimy* little boy is probably displaying courage.
    (a) underprivileged
    (b) abandoned
    (c) brave
    (d) dirty
    _____

15. The writer intended to *exclude* physical courage.
    (a) condemn
    (b) praise
    (c) leave out
    (d) emphasize
    _____

16. Benedict Arnold might have been *motivated* by a real belief in the British cause.
    (a) acting because of
    (b) acting in spite of
    (c) paid by
    (d) solicited by
    _____

17. Both people show *moral* courage.
    (a) a kind that should be approved of
    (b) a kind resting on convictions
    (c) relating to sexual abstinence
    (d) relating to the Ten Commandments
    _____

18. The non-drinker believes in *abstinence*.
    (a) moral courage
    (b) moderation
    (c) staying away from parties
    (d) refraining entirely
    _____

19. The little boy went up to his teacher and *stammered*, "Mr. Legree, I'm sorry I cheated on that test."
    (a) confessed
    (b) stuttered
    (c) spoke with difficulty and embarrassment
    (d) spoke so softly he could hardly be heard
    _____

Comprehension

Answer this multiple choice quiz according to what is said in the chapter, whether or not it agrees with your own opinion. Sometimes there is more than one right answer; if so, use the letters for *all* the right answers. Sometimes there will be *no* right answer; if so, write "none" in the blank provided.

1. Whenever someone says, "What do you mean?" he is asking for
   (a) an explanation
   (b) an argument
   (c) an account of what happened
   (d) a repeat of what you have just said
   (e) an apology

   _____

2. A good definition
   (a) includes everything anybody has ever meant by the term being defined
   (b) is definite enough to rule out everything the writer does not mean
   (c) should always be complete in a single sentence
   (d) ought not to be more than three or four words long
   (e) makes absolutely clear what the writer means when he uses the term

   _____

3. Abstract words
   (a) refer to concepts such as loyalty, patriotism, honesty, etc.
   (b) refer to things that can't be touched or seen or heard
   (c) shift their meanings from century to century
   (d) shift their meanings from speaker to speaker
   (e) are much harder to define than words that refer to physical things

   _____

4. When we say that a word is "general," we mean that
   (a) it includes a group of things
   (b) it is always more general than other words referring to members of the same group of things
   (c) it is more general than some other words referring to members of the same group of things
   (d) it should always be avoided in writing
   (e) it is usually the best choice in writing

   _____

5. When we say a word is "specific," we mean that
   (a) it includes fewer things than some other words referring to members of the same group
   (b) it is always more specific than other words referring to members of the same group
   (c) it may refer to only one thing
   (d) it may refer to a group of things, but the group is large rather than small
   (e) if it fits what you want to say, it is a better choice than a more general term

   _____

6. A generalization
   (a) is always misleading
   (b) is a statement made about a group of things or about more than one situation
   (c) is a statement that refers to only one situation
   (d) is related to an example in the same way that general words are related to specific words
   (e) is illustrated by the statement, "My cousin Effie has six toes."

   _____

7. Main idea sentences for papers of definition
   (a) are usually specific statements
   (b) are usually generalizations
   (c) are often in three parts
   (d) usually include the general class the term belongs to
   (e) seldom show how the term being defined differs from other members of the same class

   _____

8. In papers of definition, the examples used should
   (a) fit the definition
   (b) be as much alike as possible
   (c) never be used to distinguish between one thing and another that might be confused with it
   (d) be given in words as general as possible
   (e) avoid being specific

   _____

9. A good way to arrange your paragraphing is to
   (a) put all the examples in a single paragraph
   (b) make all your paragraphs of equal length
   (c) be sure that each 200-word paper has five paragraphs
   (d) give each separate point you make at least two paragraphs
   (e) begin new paragraphs at the top of each page

   _____

10. The most important thing to watch for as you revise your paper is to
    (a) begin every paragraph with a transition word such as "next," "then," "second"
    (b) use as many general words as possible
    (c) make sure that the conclusion is different from the introduction
    (d) see the paper does what the introduction promised and no more
    (e) avoid smudges and keep the margins neat

    _____

IV

Explaining:
Comparison

The kind of explanation that points out similarities or differences between two things is called *comparison*. You are comparing whenever you explain something new by contrasting it with something familiar. If you've played basketball for years but never seen a game of hockey, a comparison between the two games will help you understand what is happening when the puck goes into the net. If you have splashed around at the edge of the ocean ever since you were a baby, a comparison between ocean waves and sound waves will help you understand how sound travels.

Sometimes we make comparisons not to learn something new, but just to come to a better understanding of something already familiar to us. If you liked both *Tom Jones* and *The Graduate*, figuring out what was alike about the films and what was different increases both your understanding and your appreciation. If you're interested in popular music, comparing the social comment in a Beatles' album with the social comment in Joan Baez's songs may help you understand both performers better. Or maybe you are puzzled by the difference between what happened to Uncle Abner and what happened to Uncle Joe. They shared the same parents and milked the same cows; they hated the same high school teachers and liked the same girls. Now Uncle Abner pays taxes on twenty thousand a year and barely has time to snatch a five-dollar lunch at the Union Club. Uncle Joe lives a leisurely life on his eighty-dollar disability pension, but he isn't too disabled to wander around in the park all day, with his lunch in a brown paper bag.

And both of them claim that they like their lives. If you contrast what the two men consider important, you may end by feeling less envious of Uncle Abner, less scornful of Uncle Joe. The point to your comparison is not to condemn either one, but just to understand.

And finally, comparisons can be used as a basis for evaluating two things. The man who is trying to decide whether a thousand-dollar promotion is worth a move to Cincinnati will certainly want to make a comparison between living costs in Mudville and living costs in Cincinnati, or, if he doesn't care that much about the money, he will want to compare the schools his ten-year-old would attend. Before you buy that new car you've been saving for, you'll want a pretty careful comparison between the performance you can expect from a Toyota and what you can get from a Volkswagen. Before Tansy decided to accept the diamond Rupert's been trying to force on her finger, she made a pretty careful comparison between Rupert's economic prospects and the sure six thousand her New York agent's been promising she'll make.

Choosing a Topic

When you choose a topic for a comparison paper, consider not only *what* you will say but *why* you want to say it. It's true that almost any pairs of things are alike in some ways and different in others, but most people can figure that out for themselves. If all you're ready to say is "Elephants and mice are both similar and different," you'd better forget it; nobody can write a successful comparison by just grabbing two items out of the air and starting to make a list. You'll have better luck if you choose two things that seem at first thought to be very much alike: toads and frogs, perhaps, or the hundred-dollar gown in the Tenth Floor Salon and the bargain basement copy for $8.95. Then you go on to show that there are some pretty important differences.

Equally good comparison papers, of course, can be written by starting at the other end. Instead of choosing two things that seem alike, you can begin with a pair that most people would think entirely different and then show that there's not that much difference after all. Guppies are so small they get lost behind the seaweed, and whales so big that a swimming pool won't hold them, but they do have some things in common. Writing poems and baking cakes seem entirely different occupations, but good papers can be written showing their similarities. Whether you choose toads and frogs, guppies and whales, cheap dresses and expensive gowns, or poetry and pastry makes less difference than what you do with the comparison; the main problem is to choose a pair of things that will lead to better knowledge, better judgment, or better understanding for whoever reads your paper.

After you have chosen what you want to compare, and decided whether to emphasize similarities or differences, it's a good idea to make sure that you've left yourself enough room. In planning comparison papers, it is easy to make what you are emphasizing too narrow, to leave yourself with nothing to say. A student comparing residential areas in San Francisco with residential areas in Philadelphia, for instance, might say, "In both San Francisco and Philadelphia there are miles and miles of row houses with no separation between them, but in Philadelphia the houses are mostly of stone while in San Francisco they are usually made of wood." No matter how accurate that statement is, it will bring any writer to a dead stop; there is nowhere to go from there.

Making your topic too broad is just as dangerous. The student who says "New York City and Goodland, Kansas, are both American cities, but they are very different in many ways," could probably write for the next couple of weeks without running out of material. New York and Goodland are about as unlike as they can possibly be, in size, climate, geography, kinds of houses, methods of government, social problems, educational systems, available recreation. The list could go on and on—the topic is simply too broad.

A writer who is serious about comparing one city with another must find some kind of middle ground between nothing to say, and everything. If he is interested in housing, he might broaden his first topic by beginning, "In both San Francisco and Philadelphia there are miles and miles of row houses, but the style of architecture is quite different." Now there is something to develop. Not only can he discuss the materials used to build the houses, he can also compare their outside appearance and typical floor plans in each city.

Housing might be a good place to begin in the Goodland-New York comparison too. But because there are so many kinds of housing available in New York, the topic needs even more narrowing. One way might be to consider what $100 a month will buy in New York and what the same amount will buy in Goodland, Kansas. If you care less about where you live than about what you do when you leave your house, you might want to compare recreation in both places from the point of view of a sports enthusiast. You can *see* more games in New York; you can *play* more in Goodland. Remember, though, that the purpose is not to argue for one place or the other; the job is just to compare them.

Whatever topic you choose, your chances of writing a successful paper increase if you use material from your own experience. Students who have never visited San Francisco or Philadelphia, New York or Goodland, had better not try to write papers comparing them. Possible topics for papers of comparison are almost unlimited; your own choice is limited only by your need to choose a topic you know something about.

Exercise 1.   Here are some topics for papers of comparison. If you think a topic is all right, mark it OK. If it seems too broad, mark it "broad" and then narrow it. Be prepared to give reasons for your answers.

1. mice and men   too broad _____ OK _____

_____

2. San Francisco and New Orleans   too broad _____ OK _____

_____

3. life 100 years ago and life today   too broad _____ OK _____

_____

4. fathers and grandfathers   too broad _____ OK _____

_____

5. two kinds of jobs   too broad _____ OK _____

_____

6. two girls you know   too broad _____ OK _____

_____

7. apartments and houses   too broad _____ OK _____

_____

8. two pieces of machinery   too broad _____ OK _____

_____

9. data processing and bookkeeping   too broad _____ OK _____

_____

10. sewing and math problems   too broad _____ OK _____

___

11. helicopters and Piper Cubs   too broad _____ OK _____

___

12. Atlantic Ocean and Lake Titicaca   too broad _____ OK _____

___

13. hunting with rifles and hunting with
    bows and arrows   too broad _____ OK _____

___

14. westerns and science fiction   too broad _____ OK _____

___

15. suburbs and slums   too broad _____ OK _____

___

Exercise 2.   Here are some main idea sentences for papers of comparison. If you think a sentence is all right, mark it OK. If it seems too narrow, mark it "narrow" and rewrite it. Be prepared to give reasons for your answers.

1. Gateway Hospital charges $30 a bed; Bedlam charges $20.   _____

_____

_____

2. In Bushytail there is a big lake; in Lasso there is one swimming pool.   _____

_____

_____

3. Mary has three brothers, Maude has none.   _____

_____

_____

4. History deals with what happened; political science deals with how it happens.   _____

_____

_____

5. Chaucer lived in the 14th Century; George Bernard Shaw in the 20th.   _____

_____

_____

6. Senator Hoaxshell voted against gun registration; Senator Upright voted for it.   _____

_____

_____

Main Idea Sentences for Papers of Comparison

Once you have chosen your topic and decided why you are making the comparison, whether you want to emphasize likenesses or differences is probably already clear in your mind; your main idea sentence should help to fix it there. A good main idea sentence for a paper of comparison has two parts. The first part says what things are being compared, and the second part makes clear whether you are primarily interested in likenesses or in differences. The two parts are usually joined by such words as *although, even though, in spite of, notwithstanding,* or *but.* Using these words and phrases will help you avoid such obvious sentences as "Elephants and mice are both alike and different." You will find it much easier to make a point in your paper if you say, "*In spite of* their obvious differences, elephants and mice are very much alike in several ways."

Here are some main idea sentences that emphasize differences. Notice that the first part of each sentence tells what two things will be compared and suggests that the likenesses don't matter much; the second part says definitely that the differences do matter.

(1) Many people think that judo and karate are alike because they both originated in Japan, *but* (2) as anyone can tell you who has seen a karate expert split an oak beam with his bare hand, the art of karate is quite different from the art of judo.

(1) *Even though* grocery stores in the ghetto and the suburbs are run by the same company and go by the same name, (2) there are important differences in the choices available, the quality of the food, and the price that is charged for it.

(1) Senator Hoaxshell and Senator Upright both belong to the same political party, *but* (2) their voting records show some interesting differences.

In the following main idea sentences emphasizing likenesses, the order is reversed, and it is easy to tell that the writer will concentrate on similarities:

(1) *Notwithstanding* their wide separation in size and strength, (2) angleworms and dinosaurs have several things in common.

(1) *Although* most advertisers want you to believe there are big differences between their gasoline and all the others you can buy, (2) the ingredients that go into all gasolines are much the same.

(1) *In spite of* the contrast in salary and prestige, (2) the corporation president and the lady who scrubs his floors are alike in the ways their jobs restrict their liberty to do as they please.

Exercise 3.   Which of the following are suitable main idea sentences for comparison papers of about 500 words? If you think the sentence is unsuitable, rewrite it. If you think it is suitable, say whether the emphasis will be on likenesses or differences.

1. High school and college are both alike and different.

_____

_____

Emphasis: _____

2. Although both academic subjects and vocational subjects prepare you for life, vocational courses train you to earn your living and academic courses help you to examine and enjoy life.

_____

_____

Emphasis: _____

3. Even though most schools still keep a rigid separation between vocational and academic courses, in the long run the purpose of both courses is the same, to help you lead a better life.

_____

_____

Emphasis: _____

4. Although guppies and whales both live in the water, the way they produce and tend their young is very different.

_____

_____

Emphasis: _____

5. Even though mini-bikes and motorcycles are both motor-driven two-wheeled vehicles, there is a world of difference in speed, comfort, and handling.

_____

_____

Emphasis: _____

6. Although you may think there is a big difference between canned horse-meat and a rare filet mignon, their nourishment value is about the same.

_____

_____

Emphasis: _____

7. Minneapolis makes lots of beer whereas Detroit makes lots of cars.

_____

_____

Emphasis: _____

8. Both Tokyo and Los Angeles have populations of more than a million, but living in the two cities is not the same.

_____

_____

Emphasis: _____

9. Children in Mexico get just as excited as children in Maine about the coming of Christmas, though the way they celebrate it is not the same.

_____

_____

Emphasis: _____

10. Despite differences in flavor and effect, both vinegar and wine are made from the same things in much the same way.

_____

_____

Emphasis: _____

Exercise 4.   Write main idea sentences for papers of comparison for any five of these topics. Make some emphasize similarities and some emphasize differences. Be sure to follow the two-part pattern shown on p. 94.

1. a vacuum cleaner and a broom _____

_____

_____

_____

2. washing and dry cleaning _____

_____

_____

_____

3. Volkswagens and Jaguars _____

_____

_____

_____

4. home-made and ready-made clothes _____

_____

_____

_____

5. boys and men _____

_____

_____

_____

6. jazz and rock music _____

_____

_____

_____

7. your neighborhood and another one _____

_____

_____

_____

8. two books you have read _____

_____

_____

_____

9. two teachers you have had _____

_____

_____

_____

10. freedom and responsibility _____

_____

_____

_____

Planning the Order

Nearly all good papers begin with what the writer thinks is least important and work up to what he considers most important. Comparison papers usually follow this order, too. The main idea sentence, in fact, serves as a miniature outline. The student who is showing that corporation presidents and scrub ladies share the same restrictions will probably spend his first paragraph on the differences. He will let us see the scrub lady coming to work at 5:00 P.M. on the crowded subway just as the chauffeur drives her boss away in the corporation's black Rolls Royce. He shows everybody jumping when the president clears his throat and nobody there when the scrub lady coughs. Once the differences are taken care of, the writer will spend the rest of the paper, probably several paragraphs, explaining that the president is as tied to his gavel as the janitress is to her broom; that both of them show up on the job when they'd rather be somewhere else; that the president gets just as bored with board meetings as the scrub lady does with waste baskets. Here is the plan:

> Main idea sentence
> Differences (covered in the first paragraph)
> Similarities (rest of the paper)

For the writer who wants to emphasize differences, the main idea sentence works the same way, helping him arrange the paper so that the most important part is saved for last. The student who began by saying, "Many people think judo and karate are alike because they both originated in Japan, but as anyone can tell you who has seen a karate expert split an oak beam with his bare hand, the art of karate is quite different from the art of judo," will probably mention all the likenesses fairly early in the paper. He may say that an expert in either judo or karate must learn a good deal of physical discipline; that both skills involve a series of moves that have to be learned and practiced; that in both judo and karate the expert takes advantage of his opponent's weight and movements. The rest of the paper is left for examining the differences. The student's plan will look like this:

> Main idea sentence
> Similarities (covered in the first paragraph)
> Differences (rest of the paper)

Even though your main idea sentence can guide you in arranging the large divisions, you still must decide how you will arrange the material in the second, most important division. The order you decide on depends on the material itself. The writer comparing a ghetto grocery and a suburban grocery will probably tell everything that happens to the housewife from the time she goes through the door of the ghetto grocery until she has paid the clerk for what she bought, and then do the same for her trip to the suburban store. In the suburban account, the differences can be emphasized by phrases like, "In contrast with the scratched wooden door, . . ." "Instead of being treated . . ." "Unlike the dirty floors and broken packages, . . ." "The vegetables, instead of being bruised and wilted, . . ." The plan will look like this:

> Main idea sentence
> Similarities (covered in the first paragraph)
> Differences:
> > Everything about the ghetto grocery
> > Everything about the suburban grocery

Such a plan works well for this material because the housewife's shopping trips give a natural unity to each part, and the contrasting phrases help focus on the differences between the first store and the second, linking the two parts together.

The trouble is that not all topics fit so well into an "everything about A, then everything about B" arrangement. Unless the writer is very skillful, he risks at least three dangers: his comparison may be incomplete; his connecting phrases may be mechanical and dull-sounding; and his paper may wind up sounding like two separate essays, one on A and another on B.

In comparing judo and karate, for instance, it would be all too easy to discuss the aims of judo but forget to mention the aims of karate; to go into great detail about the special hand training in karate but to overlook whatever special training is needed for judo. If the comparison is to be complete, the two sections must balance point for point. The judo-karate topic offers nowhere near the variety of connecting phrases the grocery store paper offered, and the writer is likely to find himself saying over and over again, "In contrast, karate, . . ." and "Karate, on the other hand, . . ." Finally, it is easy to see how the writer who tries "everything about judo, everything about karate," might come up with two separate essays. Thinly disguised as a single paper, the two-in-one treatment can actually break in half rather badly, leaving the reader on his own to find the points in the first part and match them up with the points in the second.

A better method for organizing most comparison papers might be called the AB/AB/AB plan. The writer who uses this method will take up the differences point by point, comparing as he goes. Using this method, a plan for the judo-karate paper would look something like this:

Main idea sentence
Similarities (covered in first paragraph)
Differences

| Purpose: | judo is a sport |
| | karate is a serious matter |

| Aim: | judo, to throw opponent |
| | karate, to maim or kill |

| Body development: | judo, all muscles and reactions |
| | karate, certain parts developed as lethal weapons |

This type of plan helps the writer make his comparison complete and helps the reader see the contrasts.

A third possible order is a sophisticated variation of the AB/AB/AB plan. Instead of getting rid of the likenesses in the early part of the paper and then spending the rest of the paper on differences, the writer interweaves the two. Using this plan for the judo-karate comparison, the student begins *each paragraph* with likenesses and then goes on to differences:

Main idea sentence

I. Likeness: both involve a series of moves learned and practiced
   Difference: judo expert learns to throw opponent
   karate expert learns to disable him

II. Likeness: both require physical discipline
    Difference: judo expert disciplines all his muscles and works for quick reactions
    karate expert disciplines certain parts of his body until they are extremely tough

III. Likeness: in both, expert uses his opponent's weight and movements
     Difference: judo expert takes advantage of balance and gravity
     karate expert tries to break arms or legs

IV. Likeness: both often used for defense
    Difference: victim of judo expert merely thwarted
    victim of karate expert often dead

Exercise 5.   Make plans for three different papers of comparison. Make sure to use at least one main idea sentence that emphasizes differences and at least one that emphasizes similarities. This is not a reference project; choose topics you already know something about.

PLAN I (For this plan, refer to pages 100–101.)

Main idea sentence: _____

_____

_____

Similarities (or differences): _____

_____

_____

Differences (or similarities):

All about _____

    1. _____

    2. _____

    3. _____

All about _____

    1. _____

    2. _____

    3. _____

Conclusion: _____

_____

PLAN II (For this plan, refer to pages 101–102.)

Main idea sentence: _____

_____

_____

Similarities (or differences): _____

_____

_____

Differences (or similarities):

1. In _____   A. _____

_____

                                 B. _____

_____

2. In _____   A. _____

_____

                                 B. _____

_____

3. In _____   A. _____

_____

                                 B. _____

_____

Conclusion: _____

_____

PLAN III (For this plan, refer to page 102.)

Main idea sentence: _____

_____

_____

I. Likeness: _____

    Difference: A. _____

            B. _____

II. Likeness: _____

    Difference: A. _____

            B. _____

III. Likeness: _____

    Difference: A. _____

            B. _____

IV. Likeness: _____

    Difference: A. _____

            B. _____

Conclusion: _____

_____

Developing the Paper

Working out a clear plan may be the hardest part of your comparison paper, but you must also remember that the plan is no more than the bare bones. As you start to write the paper, adding ten or fifteen more points to the plan is merely adding bones to the collection, and a bag of bones is still a bag of bones. Instead, develop each point you already have; let the reader see the differences as clearly as you see them. Give some examples; put in some specific details. The writer of the judo-karate paper could just say that a karate expert develops his hands until they become lethal weapons. He will have a better paper, though, if he lets us see how the karate expert begins to toughen the side of his hand by hitting a board or table hundreds of times a day, gradually increasing the force of the blows until the hand has developed a horny pad tougher than the soles of most people's feet, building up hardness and strength until he is able to break boards, bottles, and bricks with a single stroke of his bare hand. The first sentence tells, in a general, colorless way, what the karate expert does; the second has been developed with specific details. By the time the writer has explained what the karate expert's hands can do to something as flimsy as the human body, he will have found plenty to say, and he will have said it interestingly and forcefully.

Writing the Conclusion

As you finish your paper, remember that what you want to do is compare, not praise or condemn. A single sentence summarizing the main points will do very well: "The ghetto housewife finds her choices smaller, the quality poorer, and the food more expensive." Another way is to echo the main idea: "In spite of what the advertisers tell you, once the gasoline is in your tank it makes no difference what brand it is." Or the conclusion may simply pick up the most important point and assume the reader will remember the rest: "Judo is for sport; karate is for real."

Examining a Sample Theme

Here is a student theme comparing two games:

Ping Pong and Tennis

(1)   In many ways ping pong and tennis are very much alike. The

major and most outstanding difference, of course, is the difference in size of equipment.

(2)   In ping pong, as in tennis, each player is equipped with a paddle or racket. The object of both games is to get the ball over the net and still keep the ball inside a certain area. Also, in both games, there are numerous restrictions about where the ball must be served, where the server must stand, and how the score is counted.

(3)   But also, the two games have very obvious and important differences. Of course there is a difference in size of equipment, but there is also the difference in exertion needed for each game. Table tennis, as ping pong is sometimes called, can be a very exciting and enjoyable game for almost anyone. But tennis, although exciting and enjoyable, takes much more exertion—running, jumping, etc. For this reason tennis would be limited to those persons in at least average, if not slightly better than average, health.

(4)   It would probably seem to an observer of these sports that a person who was good at tennis would also be good at ping pong. In some cases this is so, but actually it can be just the opposite. The person who stands out in tennis, for that very reason, might be horribly poor at ping pong, and vice versa. So, as a general rule it would be wise to stick to one sport or the other.

How successful is this paper? The introductory paragraph says that there are some similarities and at least one difference between ping pong and tennis, but it does not make clear whether the paper will emphasize the similarities or the differences. Does the rest of the paper concentrate on the similarities and treat the differences lightly? No, the similarities are covered in paragraph 2, and the rest of the paper, including the conclusion, discusses differences. Thus the introductory paragraph, though it does tell what two things are being compared, does not state the main idea clearly enough to focus the paper. In fact, the order of the whole paper is badly scrambled and needs reworking for both order and emphasis.

The first step is to reconstruct the main idea sentence. Since the paper apparently is intended to emphasize differences, a better main idea sentence would read:

> (1) *Although* some people think ping pong is just tennis brought indoors and greatly reduced in size, (2) anyone who has played both games knows that actually the games are quite different.

Using this new main idea sentence as a guide, the student can see that he should discuss the similarities before he deals with the differences. If he decides to put the likenesses in the second paragraph, he can keep most of paragraph 2 by making some changes. Beginning with "It is true that in ping pong, as in tennis, . . ." will give him a smoother transition. Ending the paragraph with more definite information will improve it still further:

> The rules of both games are alike in some places, too. You can play doubles—two people on each side of the net helping each other—in ping pong just as you can in tennis, and the way the players take turns serving is somewhat the same. In both games, the server gets another chance if his first ball lands in the wrong area.

Paragraph 3 will take more work because the ideas are more confused. The student doesn't really want to separate "difference in size of equipment" from "difference in exertion"; what he means is that the difference in size *results* in a difference in exertion. He might begin his third paragraph by saying, "The most obvious difference between the two games, of course, is in the size of the equipment." He might continue by explaining that the difference in the size of the balls and the rackets is less important than the size of the court on which the game is played because the ping pong player, especially if he's long of limb, can stand at one end of the table and reach most of the balls his opponent slams toward him. But the tennis player, unless he's matched with a very, very rank beginner, must run from one corner of the court to the other. By the end of an ordinary game he covers as much distance as a decathlon champion. It is this leaping and jumping that makes tennis require the extra exertion mentioned, but not really dealt with, in the first draft.

Paragraph 4 of the original paper has two major faults. First, the writer says that a "person who stands out in tennis" might be poor in ping pong "for that very reason." But being outstanding in tennis is not necessarily a *reason* for anything. We don't know why being good in tennis means being bad in ping pong until the writer explains it to us. The other fault in paragraph 4 is the last sentence, where the writer suggests that the reader "stick to one sport or the other." This advice would perhaps be a good enough conclusion for a theme of directions, but a theme of explanation ought to explain, not advise. The student should rewrite paragraph 4 to show why competence in one game doesn't insure competence in the other. He'll need to add a fifth paragraph to make his paper sound finished. Here again, the main idea sentence and the way it has been developed in the body of the theme will serve as a guide to the conclusion.

Here is the plan for the rewritten paper—a modified version of the AB/AB/AB method:

(1) Introduction: main idea sentence plus specific details

(2) Likenesses: equipment
                object of the game
                some rules

(3) Differences: size of court
> ping pong
> tennis
> exertion required
> tennis
> ping pong

(4) Differences: skill required
> tennis
> ping pong

(5) Conclusion: (most important idea) different skills required

Here is a much improved version based on this plan. Because so much of the theme has been changed, we have not underlined the new parts.

Is Table Tennis Tennis?

(1)   Although some people think ping pong is just tennis brought indoors and greatly reduced in size, anyone who has played both games knows that actually the games are quite different. All you have to do to demonstrate the differences is invite the city singles champion over for a quick game of table tennis in your newly decorated basement. If you've been practicing only since the hardware store delivered the ping pong set, you'll still show him up.

(2)   It is true that in ping pong, as in tennis, each player is equipped with a paddle or racket. The object of both games is to get the ball over the net and still make it bounce inside a certain area. The other rules of the games are alike in some places, too. You can play doubles—two people on each side of the net helping each other—in ping pong just as you can in tennis, and the way the players take turns serving is somewhat the same. In both games, the server gets another chance if his first ball lands in the wrong area.

(3)   The most obvious difference between the two games, of course, is in the size of the equipment. But the size of the balls and the rackets is less important than the size of the court on which the game is played. The ping pong player, especially if he's long of limb, can stand at one end of the table and reach most of the balls his opponent slams toward him. The tennis player, unless he's matched with a very, very rank beginner, must run from one corner of the court to the other. By the end of an ordinary game he covers as much distance as a decathlon champion. All this leaping and running and jumping makes tennis suitable only for the young and vigorous. Ping pong, although it certainly isn't a wheelchair game, can be

played by anybody with an ordinary amount of wind. Even after an hour's play, ping pong won't give him a heart attack.

(4)   The size of the court makes a difference in the way the ball is hit, too. The tennis champion may be very poor at ping pong, and the ace ping pong player may be a complete dud on the tennis court. The strength that wins a tennis game—slamming a serve as hard as he can—may make the tennis champion lose the ping pong game because he will hit the ball clear into the next room. On the other hand, the ping pong expert who stands at the center of the table returning every serve may not be able to run fast enough to reach the tennis ball when it lands in the far corner of the court.

(5)   In spite of some superficial similarities between the two games, the differences are very important. Both games require skill, but the skills they require are not the same. Table tennis, then, isn't really tennis, even though the name suggests that it might be.

Exercise 6.   On a separate sheet, write an introductory paragraph and a concluding paragraph for one of the papers of comparison you planned in Exercise 5. Be sure the introduction makes clear what you are going to do, and that the conclusion relates to the introduction and makes the paper sound finished.

Exercise 7.   Write a theme from the plan you made in Exercises 5 and 6. Before you hand it in, underline all the contrast phrases you have used.

Key Words

Here are some of the important terms used in this chapter. See whether you can answer these questions about them.

1. Name the three *uses of comparison* in everyday life, and give an example of each.
2. What are two difficulties to look out for in *narrowing a topic* for papers of comparison?
3. In papers of comparison, why is it important to emphasize either *similarities* or *differences*?
4. What are the two parts of a *main idea sentence* for a paper of *comparison*? How does the two-part main idea sentence help to show the reader that the paper will emphasize either similarities or differences?
5. How is the *order* of the paper affected by an emphasis on *similarities*? By an emphasis on *differences*?
6. Name and explain the three dangers in using the *"all about A, all about B" plan.*
7. In *developing* a paper of comparison, why is it ineffective to merely add more points to the outline? How can the paper be developed more effectively?
8. What are three acceptable ways of *concluding* a paper of comparison?

Vocabulary

The vocabulary words are given here in sentences similar to or the same as those used in the chapter. Select the meaning that fits the context best.

1. Uncle Joe lives a *leisurely* life on his pension.
   (a) fast-paced
   (b) easygoing
   (c) penny-pinching
   (d) openhanded   _____

2. She made a careful study of Rupert's economic *prospects*.
   (a) future chances
   (b) knowledge
   (c) prosperity
   (d) indebtedness   _____

3. You might want to compare it from the point of view of a sports *enthusiast*.
   (a) someone who hates sports
   (b) someone mildly interested in sports
   (c) someone very interested in sports
   (d) a star player   _____

4. Some grocery stores in the *ghetto* and in the suburb are run by the same company.
   (a) exclusive district
   (b) camp surrounded by barbed wire and armed guards
   (c) large department store
   (d) slum area   _____

5. There are contrasts in both salary and *prestige* between corporation presidents and scrub ladies.
   (a) rank and reputation
   (b) freedom and movement
   (c) determination and skill
   (d) money and property   _____

6. The main idea sentence serves as a *miniature* outline.
   - (a) enlarged to scale
   - (b) reduced to scale
   - (c) tiny
   - (d) transistorized _____

7. The president is as tied to his *gavel* as the janitress is to her broom.
   - (a) unpleasant job
   - (b) fancy desk
   - (c) gold fountain pen
   - (d) mallet

8. A judo expert must learn a good deal of physical *discipline*.
   - (a) punishment
   - (b) training
   - (c) humiliation
   - (d) obedience _____

9. The contrasting phrases help *focus* on the differences.
   - (a) concentrate on
   - (b) shine a bright light on
   - (c) cross in a lens
   - (d) provide variation on _____

10. The housewife's shopping trip will give a natural *unity* to each part.
    - (a) wholeness
    - (b) strength
    - (c) conformity
    - (d) independence _____

11. Certain parts of the body are developed as *lethal* weapons.
    - (a) harmless
    - (b) poisonous
    - (c) hard
    - (d) deadly _____

12. The victim of the judo expert is merely *thwarted*.
    - (a) foiled
    - (b) broken in two parts
    - (c) depressed
    - (d) jailed _____

13. There are numerous *restrictions* about where the ball should go.
    (a) limitations
    (b) interferences
    (c) applications
    (d) inversions _____

14. Tennis takes more *exertion*.
    (a) skill
    (b) quick reactions
    (c) physical effort
    (d) nerve _____

15. The ping pong player, especially if he's long of *limb*, can stand at one end of the table and reach most of the balls.
    (a) patience
    (b) torso
    (c) reflexes
    (d) arms and legs _____

16. His *opponent* slams balls toward him.
    (a) enemy
    (b) person playing against him
    (c) person playing with him
    (d) player equal in ability _____

17. The tennis player, unless he's matched with a very, very *rank* beginner, must run from one corner of the court to the other.
    (a) one that he belittles
    (b) absolute
    (c) flourishing
    (d) one who has been in the service _____

18. He covers as much distance as a *decathlon* champion.
    (a) a city in central Illinois
    (b) an athletic contest with ten field and track events
    (c) a track race covering ten miles
    (d) a sport which combines the steeplechase and polo _____

19. *Competence* in one game doesn't insure *competence* in the other.
    (a) ability
    (b) enjoyment
    (c) certainty of winning
    (d) eagerness to win _____

Comprehension

Answer this multiple choice quiz according to what is said in the chapter, whether or not it agrees with your own opinion. Sometimes there is more than one right answer; if so, use the letters for *all* the right answers. Sometimes there will be *no* right answer; if so, write "none" in the blank provided.

1. We often make comparisons because we want to
   (a) understand something new by contrasting it with something old
   (b) increase our understanding of two things already familiar to us
   (c) give directions on how to avoid something
   (d) provide the basis for an evaluation
   (e) blend our purposes

   _____

2. A paper of comparison
   (a) is one kind of explanation
   (b) sometimes points out differences between two similar things
   (c) sometimes points out likenesses between two different things
   (d) usually says which of two things is better than the other
   (e) usually says which of two things is worse than the other

   _____

3. A good paper of comparison will
   (a) give equal importance to both likenesses and differences
   (b) focus on either the likenesses or the differences
   (c) deal with all the differences the writer can think of
   (d) deal with only one difference if the focus is on likenesses
   (e) deal with only one likeness if the focus is on differences

   _____

4. It is important that the main idea sentence for a comparison paper not be too narrow because
   (a) each paper should contain ten or fifteen different points
   (b) the narrower a main idea sentence is, the less you have to say in the body of the paper
   (c) general statements are always more interesting
   (d) in a narrow main idea sentence, only likenesses can be dealt with
   (e) in a narrow main idea sentence, only differences can be dealt with

_____

5. Good main idea sentences for papers of comparison
   (a) usually come in two parts
   (b) usually come in three parts
   (c) are always definitions
   (d) often contain such words as "but," "even though," "although"
   (e) indicate whether likenesses or differences will be emphasized

_____

6. Which of the following would be satisfactory as a main idea sentence for a paper of comparison?
   (a) Toads and frogs can be compared.
   (b) Though they appear to be almost exactly alike, there are important differences between toads and frogs.
   (c) Mothers and teachers have some things in common, but it is the differences that make some teachers great.
   (d) New Orleans and Minneapolis are both located on the Mississippi River, but the geographical differences between them make the two cities almost completely different.
   (e) Although Volkswagens and Jaguars differ in price and appearance, they perform the same function in many of the same ways.

_____

7. If the differences are more important than the likenesses, you should
    (a) discuss the differences first
    (b) discuss the likenesses first
    (c) do a little of one, then a little of the other
    (d) dispose of the likenesses in the introductory paragraph and not refer to them again
    (e) save the differences for the concluding paragraph

    _____

8. The best way to develop a comparison paper is to
    (a) throw out the plan and start over
    (b) combine three plans already made
    (c) add ten more points to the first plan
    (d) put some meat on the bones
    (e) give examples and specific details

    _____

9. In the introductory paragraph quoted below, what is the greatest problem?

    In many ways ping pong and tennis are very much alike. The major and most outstanding difference, of course, is the difference in size of equipment.

    (a) It lacks transitions.
    (b) It indicates the wrong writing purpose.
    (c) It indicates no writing purpose.
    (d) It fails to show whether differences or likenesses will be more important.
    (e) It fails to tell what things are being compared.

    _____

10. The concluding paragraph quoted below is unsatisfactory. Why?

It would probably seem to an observer of these sports that a person who was good at tennis would also be good at ping pong. In some cases this is so, but actually it can be just the opposite. The person who stands out in tennis, for that very reason, might be horribly poor at ping pong, and vice versa. So, as a general rule it would be wise to stick to one sport or the other.

(a) It fails to explain why being good in tennis makes a person poor in ping pong.
(b) It gives advice rather than just explaining.
(c) It doesn't give enough advice on how to improve either your tennis or your ping pong game.
(d) It repeats the introduction (quoted in 9 above) almost exactly.
(e) It appears to favor tennis at the expense of ping pong.
(f) It appears to favor ping pong at the expense of tennis.

V

Explaining:
Classification

Sometimes you need to explain one term: *definition*. Sometimes you need to explain two somewhat similar terms or things: *comparison*. And sometimes you need to explain the connection between a number of things that are somehow related to each other: *classification*. You are writing a theme of classification whenever you explain things by sorting them into piles and then resorting each pile into smaller groups.

Botanists classify plant families. Zoologists classify animal families. Librarians classify books, doctors classify diseases, and lawyers classify crimes. Classification, in fact, is a method commonly used by people working in specialized fields to make their work easier and their subjects more understandable. But such specialists have no corner on classification. It's a method of explanation anybody can use, and it can be used on almost anything.

Classification and Pigeonholing

Classifying our experiences is a way of understanding them, of putting some order into what has happened to us or what we have learned. Any advance in orderly thinking is a good thing. But there is a difference between orderliness and rigidity, a difference between classifying and "pigeonholing." Pigeonholing puts a single label on things, permanently; classifying recognizes that it is useful to see relationships among groups of things, but remembers that the same groups can be classified in many different ways, from many points of view. Sorting things or people into groups is a device, not the last word.

Richard Arnold is a twenty-four-year-old college student, a Negro veteran majoring in political science. He lives with his wife two and a half miles from the college. He works from 4 to 9 P.M. as a salesman in a men's clothing store, and he voted Democratic in the last election.

This very short description shows at least ten different ways of looking at one man, at least ten different classification systems into which he would fit. Whether you classify Mr. Arnold as a husband or a veteran or a working student depends entirely on whether you are interested in finding out about the marital status, the draft status, or the employment status of college students. If you are classifying students according to income, for instance, neither Mr. Arnold's age nor his political beliefs have anything to do with it. Whatever classification system you use will leave out some of the "real Mr. Arnold"; it has to, because the system is set up from a single point of view, for one purpose, and for one time.

Pigeonholing, on the other hand, gets hold of one detail and thinks it has the whole Mr. Arnold. Instead of remembering that there are other systems by which he could be classified, it assumes that he can be placed permanently in a single group. Pigeonholing keeps us from thinking clearly; honest classification clears things up.

Finding a Topic

Almost any group of things—or ideas or people—that interests you is a possible topic for classification. Cars or clothes; jobs or jewelry; furniture, foods, or fads—it doesn't really matter. What you decide to classify makes less difference than what you do with it.

Take college students, for example. They can be classified according to income, size, grade-point average, age, activities, popularity, or even their reasons for coming to college, and that list doesn't begin to use up all the possibilities. The system you choose depends on what you know about students and what you think your readers may be interested in. If you are writing for the registrar who is hoping to raise the tuition, you can classify students by income and show how many will be unable to come back next term if costs are raised. You can classify students by activities, if you're interested in how they spend their time, or which activities draw the most students, or which students are most involved. Whichever system you choose, choose it because it will provide information, or make something clearer and easier to understand. In other words, choose both your topic and your method of classifying so your paper will make a point.

Exercise 1. List at least three points of view from which each of these topics could be classified.

EXAMPLE: movies
1. violent and non-violent
2. educational and commercial
3. adult and juvenile

1. washing machines (1) _____

(2) _____

(3) _____

2. hospital patients (1) _____

(2) _____

(3) _____

3. books (1) _____

(2) _____

(3) _____

4. wines (1) _____

(2) _____

(3) _____

5. wives (1) _____

(2) _____

(3) _____

6. policemen (1) _____

(2) _____

(3) _____

7. boats   (1) _____

                (2) _____

                (3) _____

8. pianists   (1) _____

                (2) _____

                (3) _____

9. transportation   (1) _____

                (2) _____

                (3) _____

10. buildings   (1) _____

                (2) _____

                (3) _____

11. humor   (1) _____

                (2) _____

                (3) _____

12. propaganda   (1) _____

                (2) _____

                (3) _____

Main Idea Sentences for Papers of Classification

The main idea sentence for a classification paper will show the direction your paper will take, but it can't serve as a model outline as easily as do main idea sentences for papers of definition or comparison. In classification, your main idea sentence shows where you will begin, not where you will end. A good main idea sentence will tell what is being classified (the topic); what method of explanation the paper will use (classification); and the point of view your paper will take (what the first division will be based on).

Here are some main idea sentences for papers of classification:

Students come to college for five reasons: to play on a team; to marry; to avoid the draft; to learn a profession; and to get a general education.
(1) topic: students
(2) point of view: reasons for coming to college

The durability of clothing depends on the material it is made from: cotton, wool, and synthetics.
(1) topic: clothing
(2) point of view: durability of materials

Professional football players can be put into three categories: smart, fast, or beefy.
(1) topic: professional football players
(2) point of view: kinds of ability

All these main idea sentences show the direction the paper will take. Because they have a clear point of view they are likely to lead to papers that make a point.

Exercise 2.   If these sentences are suitable as main ideas for papers of classification, mark them OK. If they are unsuitable, say why.

1. Students at Shady Oak can be divided into three groups, men, women, and veterans.

_____

_____

2. The science fiction books I have read could be classified as pure fantasy.

_____

_____

3. So-called "bad words" can be divided into three categories: vulgarity, profanity, and obscenity.

_____

_____

4. Political candidates can be grouped by age, sex, and popularity.

_____

_____

5. Political candidates can be considered according to the offices they are running for: local, state, or national.

_____

_____

6. American zoos fall into two divisions, those with money enough to afford elephants and those without.

_____

_____

7. There are several ways to classify TV shows.

_____

_____

8. The violence on TV shows this year is not as shocking as it was last
year.

_____

_____

9. Zoologists divide living creatures into two groups, vertebrates and non-
vertebrates.

_____

_____

10. My neighbors are all gossips, nosy old women, or elderly snoops.

_____

_____

Exercise 3.   Write a main idea sentence for a paper of classification for any ten of these topics.

1. pets _____

_____

_____

2. deserts _____

_____

_____

3. hobbies _____

_____

_____

4. apartments _____

_____

_____

5. teachers _____

_____

_____

6. love _____

_____

_____

7. airplanes _____

_____

_____

8. neckties _____

_____

_____

9. purses _____

_____

_____

10. museums _____

_____

_____

11. politicians _____

_____

_____

12. methods of housecleaning _____

_____

_____

13. summer jobs _____

_____

_____

Planning the Paper

If you decide to write on the general topic of movies, spend some time thinking about the different large classes movies can be divided into. For example, here are some of the ways movies might be divided:

> adult and juvenile
> fictional and documentary
> art and commercial
> serious and escapist
> violent and nonviolent

Obviously, if your first division is "adult and juvenile," you are going to say different things about films than you would if you started with "art and commercial." This first division will establish the system that the rest of your paper will follow.

Suppose you decide to use "violent and nonviolent" as the first step in your classification. Your main idea sentence might be, "Although movies offer more variety now than they ever have before, probably all of them can be classified as either violent or nonviolent."

Classifying violent films into two kinds, physical and psychological, appears to include all violent movies. If you can think of one or two, however, that seem to combine these kinds of violence, perhaps you need another category: a combination.

So far your plan looks like this:

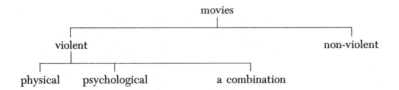

As you write your introduction, you'll need to define your key term and give some examples of what it is and what it isn't:

> Either a film gives you a tremendous shock or it doesn't. Conventional notions of violence don't always apply. For instance, in *Peter Pan* we find a sinister crocodile, a maimed and bloodthirsty pirate, and a tribe of Indians bent on kidnapping. However, none of these things shocks us deeply; instead, they are the amusing background of an entertaining fantasy, and *Peter Pan* cannot therefore be considered a violent movie.

When what you mean by violence has been cleared up, you can go on to explain the difference between physical and psychological violence:

> One gets its effect by powerful and shocking deeds happening before your eyes; the other shocks by the implications of those deeds. Physical violence is shooting and bashing and gore; psychological violence is a woman frightened to death. Physical violence stays on the surface; psychological violence explores emotional depths.

Your third step will be to give examples of movies which are physically violent and those which are psychologically violent. *Bonnie and Clyde, Dr. No,* and *In Cold Blood* will all fit the first group; *Psycho, The Stranger,* and *Whatever Happened to Baby Jane?* will illustrate the second. By the time you've explained how and why each of the examples belongs in its assigned group, your paper will be written, and you will also have done some interesting and original thinking about a part of your experience you may have taken for granted until now.

In the conclusion you can point out that some films offer both physical and psychological violence—*The Pawnbroker* and *Crime and Punishment,* for instance—but that most movies will fall into one category or the other.

Making a Classification Chart

Now that we have described one possible direction a paper classifying movies might take, we can quite easily make a chart showing exactly how we subdivided the general group:

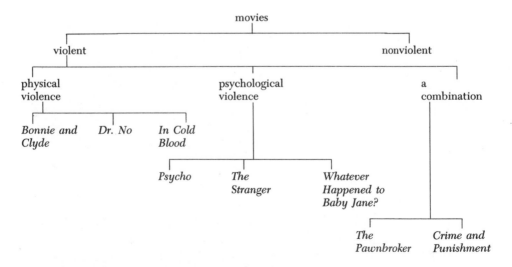

Chart 1

Although one use of classification charts is to sort out your own thoughts before you begin to write, a classification system can also help to sort out information you have been given. A chart of writing purposes, as they have been presented in this book, would look like this:

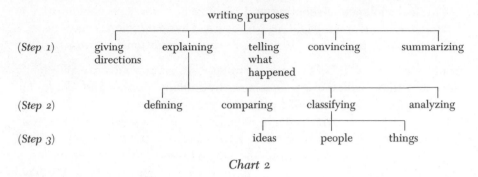

Chart 2

Because at the moment we are especially interested in classification, we did not subdivide all the categories in the first step, nor in the second step. Notice, however, that we did not jump from the first step to the third; it would be misleading to go from "explaining" directly to "kinds of people or ideas." Instead, the chart shows that classifying is one kind of explanation, and that classification of ideas or classification of people or classification of things are subgroups. Although a chart like this might be primarily useful in straightening out what you have learned so far in this course, it also might serve as a writing plan if you were answering a test question about writing purposes.

Exercise 4. Choose two of the main idea sentences from Exercise 3 and make classification charts which take at least three steps. See the charts on pp. 129–130 for samples. If the chart you make doesn't fit your original main idea sentence, keep the chart and rewrite the sentence. After you have made the chart, the first step or two may seem unnecessary; in that case, chop off what you don't need and begin with your narrowed subject.

1. Main idea sentence: _____

_____

Step 1:

Step 2:

Step 3:

2. Main idea sentence: _____

_____

Step 1:

Step 2:

Step 3:

Examining a Sample Theme

The Bookstore

(1)   "Hey, Sam! There's a bookstore. Let's go buy a book or two. Maybe we can impress the gang." So the two boys wandered into the bookstore and stopped about two feet inside the door, astonished and confused by the collection of reading material spread out in front of them. "How are we going to find anything in all this mess?" Sam asked.

(2)   But soon one of the boys saw a sign marked TEXTBOOKS. He glanced in that direction, saw a copy of his history book, *Through the Ages with the Sages,* shuddered, and turned toward the other sign: LEISURE READING. "Hey, let's go look at these paperbacks. 'Leisure' means 'fun,' doesn't it? If we're going to buy books, we may as well enjoy it."

(3)   In the leisure reading section there were still more signs: FICTION and NONFICTION. Sam thought nonfiction would be more impressive, but he took one glance at Hobbes' *Leviathan* and decided he wasn't up to it. Moving over to the fiction racks, he found still more signs: CLASSICS and CONTEMPORARY. Still hoping to find something that would look impressive, they examined a few classics. But Sam had read some Cooper in the eighth grade, and he decided fairly quickly that *The Last of the Mohicans* was not his idea of leisure reading. They went on to the contemporary section.

(4)   There the signs offered a choice among SCIENCE FICTION, MYSTERIES, HISTORICAL NOVELS, WESTERNS, and HUMOR. The two boys saw and discarded *Marooned on the New Moon, Who Killed Rock Cobbin? The Last Days of Bombay,* and *Custer's Next-to-Last Stand.* That left HUMOR. But even here there were signs. Sam decided, after one look at *Why Bigamy Is Preferable to Bachelorhood,* that he didn't want SATIRE, so they went on to SLAPSTICK. Here, at last, Sam found a book that he thought he might enjoy. He hauled out his nickels and dimes and pennies and bought a copy of *I Lost My Mother-in-Law in a Bookstore.*

(5)   "Gee, I'm not surprised the old girl got lost," Sam said as they left. "If they didn't have some kind of system, nobody could ever find anything in there!"

If you look for a main idea sentence in the first paragraph of this theme, you will not find it. Nevertheless, the student who wrote this paper did have a clear main idea sentence in his head, and if you look back at the first paragraph, you can make a fairly good guess at what it was. By the time you have read the whole theme, you should be able to work it out yourself: *Books can be classified into two main divisions, textbooks and books for leisure reading.*

Although the writer has not stated his main idea, he has used his introduction to gain interest. Watching two boys discover a classification system makes for livelier reading than simply being told what the system is. In spite of beginning with conversation, however, this introduction does serve as a contract. The introduction makes it clear enough that the paper will try to make order from the confusing array of books. If the rest of the paper did not classify the books into some kind of system, the reader would feel cheated.

Beginning with conversation implies another promise, too. The reader expects to be told a story, and he is told one. In other words, the writer has blended telling what happened with explaining, but he never lets his eagerness to tell a story interfere with his main purpose, classifying books. And although he maintains the same tone by ending, as he began, with quoted conversation, he uses the quotation to restate his main point: the bookstore's classification system helps the purchaser find books. This repetition of the main point makes the paper sound finished.

In spite of the lively and informal writing, this theme succeeds in following the assignment clearly and well. It is easy to make a classification chart showing the system that has been followed (see Chart 3). Notice that the student has taken only one step at a time and that each subdivision includes all the members of the group it subdivides.

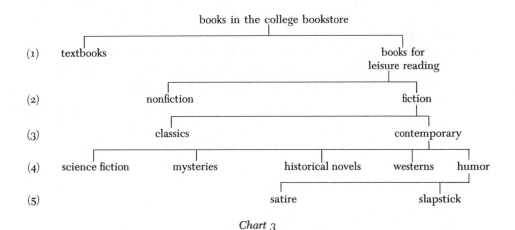

Chart 3

Exercise 5.   The following theme of classification has its sentences scrambled. Rearrange the sentences into a complete well-ordered theme, containing an introduction, a body, and a conclusion. If you have kept each point in its own paragraph, you should come out with six paragraphs.

Traveling by car, however, is tiring, and the driver runs the risk of falling asleep at the wheel if he is traveling alone. People who want to get from Portland, Oregon, to San Francisco have a choice of four methods: car, bus, plane, or train. A few years ago there was a boat, too, but now the regular passenger boats no longer run and the only water travel is by private motorboat or by freighter. The bus is the cheapest method, but buses offer very little in the way of sightseeing, and the trip can become very boring. Airplanes are by far the fastest method of travel, but they are also by far the most expensive. Since the freighters run for their convenience rather than for the convenience of the passengers, neither motorboat nor freighter is practical enough to be considered. The train trip is more expensive than the bus ride, and less expensive than the plane trip. Meals at bus stops are hurried and not very good. The man who goes by private car can leave whenever he wishes, travel as fast as the law and his own state of exhaustion will allow, and choose whatever route suits his fancy. Each of these methods of travel has its own advantages and its own drawbacks. If the traveler has money to burn, and is not put off by death statistics, he will choose the plane trip. Moreover, the traveler whose legs stiffen when he sits in one position for several hours may find the bus ride very uncomfortable. The traveler must decide whether he values speed, economy, sightseeing, or comfort, and make his choice accordingly. Trains travel through the high mountains and offer their passengers dazzling varieties of natural scenery. Then all he has to do is fill his gas tank or buy his ticket, and the slowest of these methods will get him to San Francisco in less than twenty-four hours. Cramped legs can be stretched by a walk down the aisle and the food is usually good, though expensive, on a train.

Exercise 6. Make a classification chart showing the divisions and subdivisions in the paper you rearranged in Exercise 5.

Exercise 7. Write an introductory paragraph and a concluding paragraph for a paper of classification, using one of the topics you have already outlined. Be sure the introduction tells the reader what you are going to classify and that the conclusion relates to the introduction and makes the paper sound finished.

Exercise 8. Write a theme from the plan you made for Exercises 4 and 7. Remember that for each step in the chart and for each subdivision in the final step you will probably need a separate paragraph. Before you hand in your theme, underline all the transitions between paragraphs.

Key Words

Here are some of the important terms used in this chapter. See whether you can answer these questions about them.

1. How does *classification* differ from definition or comparison?

2. What is the difference between *classifying* and *pigeonholing?*

3. Once you have decided on a topic, how should you decide which *classification system* to use?

4. What should a *main idea sentence* for a *classification* paper contain?

5. If the main idea sentence cannot serve as a model outline, what does it show about the *development* of the paper?

6. What two *uses* does a *classification chart* have for a college student?

7. FOR DISCUSSION: Can you see any connection between being able to *classify* and being able to recognize and identify relationships between things or people?

Vocabulary

The vocabulary words are given here in sentences similar to or the same as those used in the chapter. Select the meaning that fits the context best.

1. The *zoologist* uses classification in his work.
   (a) someone who studies zoos
   (b) someone who organizes libraries
   (c) someone who studies plants
   (d) someone who studies animals   _____

2. There is a difference between orderliness and *rigidity*.
   (a) messiness
   (b) flexibility
   (c) inflexibility
   (d) cleanliness   _____

3. He can be classified according to his *marital* status.
   (a) service in the armed forces
   (b) married or unmarried
   (c) merit pay
   (d) number of demerits   _____

4. He can be classified according to his draft *status*.
   (a) condition
   (b) prestige
   (c) feelings
   (d) board   _____

5. The *durability* of clothing depends on the material.
   (a) appearance
   (b) price
   (c) resistance to wear
   (d) comfort   _____

6. Most clothing is made from cotton, wool, or *synthetics*.
   (a) chemical rather than natural
   (b) natural rather than chemical
   (c) not real or genuine
   (d) a cheap imitation   _____

7. Movies might be divided into fictional and *documentary.*
   (a) mostly in written form
   (b) dealing with actual events
   (c) highly imaginative
   (d) arguing against something   _____

8. Movies might be divided into art and *commercial.*
   (a) intended to sell a certain idea or product
   (b) full of advertising breaks
   (c) produced to make money
   (d) never really good   _____

9. Movies might be divided into serious and *escapist.*
   (a) full of slapstick comedy
   (b) unlike actual experience
   (c) highly realistic
   (d) dealing with criminals and police trying to
       capture them   _____

10. Your first division may include *juvenile* movies.
    (a) concerned with delinquency
    (b) rowdy and ill-behaved
    (c) intended for the young
    (d) intended for social outcasts   _____

11. *Conventional* notions of violence don't always apply.
    (a) generally agreed on
    (b) established by a large group of delegates during
        a public meeting
    (c) scheming
    (d) uncommonly cruel   _____

12. In *Peter Pan* we find a *sinister* crocodile.
    (a) badly injured
    (b) ominously evil
    (c) extremely sinful
    (d) very bloodthirsty   _____

13. They are the amusing background of an entertaining *fantasy.*
    (a) imaginary story
    (b) lie
    (c) nightmare
    (d) ghostly vision   _____

14. Most movies will fall into one *category* or the other.
    (a) index
    (b) price range
    (c) group
    (d) system _____

15. In this section there were two more signs, *fiction* and non-fiction.
    (a) written in prose, without rhythm or rhyme
    (b) poetry, not prose
    (c) a story of something that didn't actually happen
    (d) anything that's fun to read _____

16. He found still more signs: classics and *contemporary*.
    (a) produced in modern times
    (b) halfway between classical and modern
    (c) beneath respect
    (d) having to do with meditation and deep thought _____

17. After one look at *Why Bigamy Is Preferable to Bachelorhood*, he decided he didn't want satire.
    (a) a dwarf-like native of Africa
    (b) a big spender
    (c) having more than one wife
    (d) having more than one mammy _____

18. After one look at *Why Bigamy Is Preferable to Bachelorhood*, he decided he didn't want *satire*.
    (a) any funny writing
    (b) writing that ridicules or exaggerates
    (c) writing that presents Aristotelian logic
    (d) writing that deals with domestic problems _____

19. The paper will try to make order from the confusing *array* of books.
    (a) display
    (b) jumble
    (c) bargain table
    (d) floor-to-ceiling shelving _____

20. Beginning with conversation *implies* another promise.
    (a) suggests
    (b) contradicts
    (c) denies
    (d) emphasizes _____

Comprehension

Answer this multiple choice quiz according to what is said in the chapter, whether or not it agrees with your own opinion. Sometimes there is more than one right answer; if so, use the letters for *all* the right answers. Sometimes there will be *no* right answer; if so, write "none" in the blank provided.

1. A paper that explains the relationship between a number of things in a group is called
   (a) definition
   (b) comparison
   (c) classification
   (d) analysis
   (e) argument

   _____

2. For most topics
   (a) there is only one system of classification
   (b) there are usually several ways of classifying
   (c) there are always two ways to classify
   (d) it is better to change systems at the third step
   (e) it is better to keep the same system throughout your paper

   _____

3. The difference between classifying and pigeonholing is that pigeonholing
   (a) puts a single label on things and thinks it is permanent
   (b) keeps us from thinking clearly
   (c) helps us to think more clearly
   (d) gets hold of one detail and assumes it is the whole
   (e) is a better and more complete system than classifying

   _____

4. When choosing a system of classification for your topic,
   (a) choose the one that deals with it chronologically
   (b) choose the one that deals with it causally
   (c) move from heaviest to lightest
   (d) use whatever method will help you make your point
   (e) use the only method that the topic will allow

   _____

5. The main idea sentence for a paper of classification
   (a) cannot serve as a model outline as some other main idea sentences do
   (b) shows where you will begin
   (c) shows where you will end
   (d) should tell what the topic is
   (e) should make clear what the purpose of the paper is

   _____

6. The first division of a classification chart
   (a) is less important than the rest
   (b) is more important than the rest
   (c) establishes the system the rest of the chart will follow
   (d) must include everything in the original group
   (e) must include most of what was in the original group

   _____

7. In making a classification chart, it is important to
   (a) get from the general topic to the final step as fast as you can
   (b) take only one step at a time
   (c) combine steps whenever you can
   (d) never take more than three steps at a time
   (e) as you take a step, never leave out anything that has been in the previous step

   _____

8. The sample student paper which classified books in the bookstore
   (a) was lively and informal
   (b) was formal and traditional
   (c) failed to sort books into groups
   (d) failed to mention specific books
   (e) used examples effectively

   _____

9. The following is the introduction to the student paper of classification on books in a bookstore. Which of the statements about it are true?

   "Hey, Sam! There's a bookstore. Let's go buy a book or two. Maybe we can impress the gang." So the two boys wandered into the bookstore and stopped about two feet inside the door, astonished and confused by the collection of reading material spread out in front of them. "How are we going to find anything in all this mess?" Sam asked.

   (a) It is unsuccessful because it does not state a main idea sentence.
   (b) It gains interest by using conversation.
   (c) It serves as a contract agreeing to make order out of the confusing assortment of books.
   (d) It is misleading and dull.
   (e) It promises to blend telling what happened with classifying.

   _____

10. In the sample theme, "The Bookstore,"
    (a) all the books mentioned are real
    (b) all the books mentioned are made up
    (c) some are real books and some are imaginary
    (d) all the books are fiction
    (e) all the books are nonfiction

    _____

VI

Explaining:
Analysis

The fourth method of explaining is analysis. Things that cannot be defined or compared or classified can often be explained by analysis: explaining a whole thing by examining it piece by piece. Although both classification and analysis deal with separate things that somehow belong together, classification usually subdivides, labels each subdivision, and then subdivides again, and perhaps again; analysis, on the other hand, usually examines the separate working parts of a single thing or the separate causes of a single event. We *classify* kinds of automobiles; we *analyze* the working parts of an internal combustion engine. We *classify* possible causes of motor failure; we *analyze* the reasons one particular car won't run.

Operational Analysis

You can best explain how a carburetor works by examining the relationship of the mixing chamber, the air intake, the gas intake, and the jet that regulates the proper proportion of gas and air. You can explain how blood courses through the human body by analyzing the parts of the circulatory system: the heart, the arteries, the veins, and the lungs. You can explain how a proposal to stop dogs barking is transformed into a state law by discussing the part played by the doghater who wrote the bill, the clerk who gave it a number, the committee that reviewed it, the anti-dog people who lobbied for it, the legislators that voted on it, and the governor who finally signed it into law. In explaining any of these things—the carburetor, the blood system, and the silent-dog law—your concern is not whether they *should* happen that way, but only in understanding how they *do* happen; you explain what the process is. Because such explanations deal with *how something works,* they are often called *operational analysis.*

Causal Analysis

Sometimes, however, you want to find out, not *how* something works, but *why* it turned out the way it did. You can explain the alarming expense of a wedding by analyzing the cost of providing the bridesmaids' dresses, paying the minister's fee, renting the tuxedos, paying a singer and an accompanist, buying the cake and punch, and hiring somebody to serve the food and a janitor to clean up the mess. The parts, taken together, explain the whole. You can explain the failure of the local recreation bonds if you analyze both the events and the attitudes that led to the failure. It rained two inches on election day, and many people thought dry feet were more important than a new municipal swimming pool. Not enough publicity was given to the election; many people, the day after, didn't even know the election had been held. On the ever-important question of money, probably too much emphasis was given to the five-dollar tax increase on a house valued at ten thousand dollars, and too little attention to the probable decrease of money spent on juvenile authorities and detention homes. Too many people who could afford swimming pools in their own backyards forgot about the people who couldn't, and too many people who couldn't afford them thought swimming pools were foolishness anyway. All these elements, taken together, caused the bond issue to fail. Any analysis that looks for the causes of some event, that tries to find out why it happened, is called *causal analysis.*

Although both operational and causal analysis explain something by examining the separate parts, operational analysis explains a process that works the same way over and over again; causal analysis tries to explain why one event, or two or three similar events, occurred. For instance, analyzing the relationship between heart, veins, arteries, and lungs is an operational analysis because it explains a process that normally goes on inside all of us, minute after minute and day after day. If the blood stops circulating, however, an attempt to explain why it stopped, in that one body at that one time, is causal analysis, just as an examination of what happened when the carburetor stopped producing the proper mixture in your MG yesterday at 2:15 would be an attempt to find out, not *how,* but *why.*

Analysis can range from the very simple to the very complex. Operational analysis becomes progressively complicated as more elements are introduced, but it is still fairly simple because it focuses on a repeated process. To explain how a carburetor works is easier than explaining the circulatory system; the circulatory system is simpler than the process of getting a bill through the state legislature. The most complicated operational analysis, however, is likely to be simpler than the causal analysis of even a quite ordinary event, because in causal analysis you have to find the parts for yourself and decide how important each part is. Finding the four or five reasons your girl friend won't speak to you is doubtless easier than discovering why the local recreation bonds failed; but analyzing the bond failure may be child's play compared to the job undertaken by the President's commission on riots. In causal analysis, too, the difficulties are relative to the complexity of the situation.

Notice, however, that all these causal analyses limit themselves to finding out *why* something happened; they do not protest that it should not have happened that way, or argue for better conditions. The paper analyzing the cost of the wedding does not maintain that the minister, or the janitor, charged too much. Finding out why your girl won't speak to you is not the same as getting her to make up, and discovering why the recreation bonds didn't pass is not the same as arguing for or against their passage. The bonds *didn't* pass because it rained, because there was too little publicity about the election and too much emphasis on how much the new pool would cost. If the writer goes beyond analysis into argument, he will leave the rain out of it, because he can't control that anyway, and, if he is against the bonds, he will argue that Jones and Brown ought not to pay for a swimming pool for Johnson's kids; if he's for the bond issue, he'll argue that we shouldn't worry about money when genuine community improvement is the real issue. Whether he's for or against, however, his argument will deal with his reasons for thinking something *ought to* happen; his analysis is concerned with why it *did* happen. Argument takes sides; analysis doesn't. Argument looks to the future (*ought to* or *should*); operational analysis looks to the present (*how*), and causal analysis to the past (*why*). And even though argument sometimes makes use of analysis, it's useful to keep the two things separate. Whether it is as simple as how a carburetor works, or as complex as why Watts happened, analysis is an important kind of explanation.

Main Idea Sentences for Analysis

Because any kind of analysis explains the whole by explaining the relationship of the parts, a satisfactory main idea sentence must show what the whole is and what parts (or perhaps how many) make up the whole:

A carburetor (*the whole*) cannot operate unless it has a mixing chamber, an air intake, a gas intake, and a jet (*the parts*).

The circulatory system (*the whole*) is composed of the heart, the arteries, the veins, and the lungs (*the parts*).

A bill becomes a state law (*the whole*) only after it has gone through six separate stages (*the parts*).

Everything about a wedding costs money (*the whole*), from buying the bridesmaids' dresses to hiring someone to clean up when it is all over (*the parts*).

The recreation bonds failed to pass (*the whole*) for three reasons: because of the weather, the amount and kind of publicity, and the attitudes of individual voters (*the parts*).

The patient's death (*the whole*) can be attributed to his advanced age, his weakened condition, the strenuous gymnastic exercises he was performing, and the amount of rum he had just drunk (*the parts*).

It's easy enough to tell that the first three of these sample main idea sentences will lead to papers of operational analysis. In each, the notion of a function or a process is either stated or implied. The last three main idea sentences will lead to causal analysis; two of them actually contain the word *because*, and the other one hints at it. An even easier way to recognize them as causal, however, is that in each of them the *whole* is a single event, not a recurring process.

Most of these main idea sentences also give some clue as to the order the paper will follow. The carburetor paper will probably begin with the mixing chamber and end with the jet; the paper on the circulatory system apparently will start with the heart. Although the order that will be followed in analyzing the high cost of getting married is not quite as obvious, probably the writer plans to begin with the most expensive item (the bridesmaids' dresses) and work his way down to the least expensive (paying the janitor). If he means to do it the other way round, his main idea sentence should read: "Everything about a wedding costs money, from the ten dollars the janitor charges to the hundred-dollar gowns the bridesmaids wear." The paper explaining how a bill becomes law will follow the same order as the bill, from the first step in the process to the last one; the two papers showing why something happened (why the bonds failed, why the old man died) will probably move from the least important cause to the most important.

Exercise 1.   Examine these main idea sentences to see whether they are suitable for a paper of operational analysis, causal analysis, directions, or argument, and be prepared to defend your decision in class. For operational analysis, write *OA*, for causal *CA*, for directions *D*, and for argument *A*.

1. Rupert's failing math seemed to result from three things, that he didn't buy a book, he never went to class, and he thought seven times eight was fifty-two.   _____

2. The old opera house collapsed because there were termites in the foundation, the city had no funds to repair it, and the capacity audience clapped rhythmically and stamped their feet when the jug band played.

    _____

3. The state ought to repair the old opera house and make it into a historical monument.   _____

4. Any good paper must have three parts, a beginning, a middle, and an end.   _____

5. The easiest way to write a good paper is to decide what your main point will be, finish the main part of the paper, and then write a beginning and an end that fit what you have said.   _____

6. An ordinary cigarette lighter has four working parts: flint, ratchet wheel, wick, and fuel reservoir.   _____

7. A guitar has six parts: fingerboard, strings, tuning pegs, bridge, anchor, and soundbox.   _____

8. To tune a guitar, you must follow several steps.   _____

9. A piano affords a musician more range of effect and expression than any other instrument.   _____

10. There are four reasons that electrically amplified guitars are more pleasing to listen to than classical guitars are.   _____

11. The youngest child in a family has four pressures working on him nearly all the time.   _____

12. Being the youngest child in a family is better than being the oldest.

         _____

13. Four factors contributed to the Wall Street crash of 1929.   _____

14. To change your social status, there are three steps to follow.   _____

15. Like the man who wrote *Black Like Me*, everyone should be a Negro for at least a month.   _____

16. It is better to be in the social majority for three excellent reasons.

         _____

17. The peculiarities of the English spelling system result from a set of historical changes.   _____

18. There are four reasons for the hippies' rejection of conventional values.

         _____

Exercise 2. Write main idea sentences for papers of analysis on any five of these topics. Do not have all causal or all operational, but use some of each.

1. a coffee pot (any kind) _____

_____

_____

2. a hair dryer _____

_____

_____

3. a door lock _____

_____

_____

4. a dress pattern _____

_____

_____

5. a thermometer (any kind) _____

_____

_____

6. a car jack _____

_____

_____

7. the expenses of a summer trip _____

_____

_____

8. the cost of going to Europe _____

_____

_____

9. a television series show, such as "Bonanza" or "Peyton Place" _____

_____

_____

_____

10. why you got an *A* (or an *F*) in some course you have taken _____

_____

_____

_____

11. your relationship with some member of your family _____

_____

_____

_____

12. a causal analysis of something with which you are familiar—something

   important and real _____

_____

_____

_____

Examining a Sample Theme

How a Camera Works

Most people think that cameras are hard to understand because they often see a lot of lenses, flash attachments, tripods, and other fancy gadgets which are sold with cameras. However, all cameras work on the same principle, and the gadgets are merely extras. If you analyze the four parts of a simple box camera you will discover exactly how a $500 imported job works—the principle is the same, only the extras are different.

First there is a light-proof box which holds the film. It can be a fancy camera or an old shoe box, just as long as it keeps the light out. The inside of the box has to be completely dark or else the film may be spoiled and come out streaked or completely blank.

Next is the film. In most cameras the film is rolled across one end of the camera, but it doesn't have to be. It can be just a single piece of film taped to one side of a light-proof shoe box. The film must not be exposed to light before the picture is taken.

Third is the lens, or opening. This is on the side of the box opposite the film, and it is through the hole that the light comes to hit the film and expose it.

Fourth and last is the shutter, which opens and closes the lens or opening. Obviously you can't leave the opening uncovered all the time or else you would expose your film before you were ready to, and would probably ruin the picture.

Thus we see how the four parts work. The shutter opens and lets light through the lens and onto the film in the dark box. The lens is covered and the picture has been taken. As for the difference between my shoe box camera and the fancy model? You'll have to ask the man who sells them. I don't understand it myself.

Notice that although this theme (an operational analysis) explains the process by which any camera works, the writer is not telling the reader how to build a camera or even how to take pictures. If the writer had done either of those things, he would have written a paper of directions. The difference between analysis and directions should be clear if you compare the second paragraph of "How a Camera Works" with this paragraph from a theme called "How to Build a Simple Camera."

To build a simple box camera you will need a sturdy shoe box, some heavy wrapping paper, a roll of masking tape, an ordinary pin, and a small piece of cardboard. To operate the camera, you will also need a roll of film of any size.

The first step is to . . .

Next you . . .

The writer who knows what his purpose is will be better able to stick to giving directions, if that is what he means to do, or to analyzing, if he means to explain.

The first paragraph of "How a Camera Works" clearly states the purpose: an analysis of cameras to explain how they work. The main idea sentence with which the writer probably started (All cameras work with just four parts) has been broken up and made part of two sentences, but the whole idea is clearly there. Further, the main paragraph catches the reader's attention by telling why the paper is being written: to remove some of the confusion about cameras.

Does the order of the parts analyzed seem clear? It seems so to us, since the parts are presented in much the same way that we load, then use a camera: starting with the box, then the film, then the operation of the shutter. This order is made even more clear through the use of transitions. Notice how the paragraphs are introduced, from paragraph 2 on through the theme: *First . . . Next . . . Third . . . Fourth . . . Thus. . . .*

Does the conclusion make the paper sound finished? It does, both by summing up the analysis that has already been given, and by referring back to the introduction and picking up the idea that was introduced earlier—that the principle applies to all cameras. Further, the writer repeats the comparison of the shoe box and the $500 camera. This repeating not only finishes the theme, but it also ties the whole thing together very nicely.

Exercise 3.　　　Choose two main idea sentences from Exercise 2, one causal and one operational, and for each of them make a plan that can be developed into a paper. This is not a reference project; choose topics you already know something about. Be sure you can defend the order of each part in your plans.

Analysis of: _____

Introduction (*use your main idea sentence here*): _____

_____

_____

_____

1. _____

_____

_____

2. _____

_____

_____

3. _____

_____

_____

Conclusion (*use a variation of your main idea sentence here*): _____

_____

_____

_____

Analysis of: _____

Introduction (*use your main idea sentence here*): _____

_____

_____

_____

1. _____

_____

_____

2. _____

_____

_____

3. _____

_____

_____

4. _____

_____

_____

Conclusion (*use a variation of your main idea sentence here*): _____

_____

_____

_____

Exercise 4. For both the plans you made in Exercise 3, write introductory and concluding paragraphs. Be sure the introduction tells the reader what you are going to analyze and makes clear whether your analysis will be operational or causal. Check your conclusion to make sure that it avoids argument.

Exercise 5. Write a theme from one of the plans you made in Exercises 3 and 4. Remember, after breaking the whole down into pieces, to show how each part relates to the whole. Before you hand in your theme, underline all the transitions between paragraphs.

Key Words

Here are some of the important terms used in this chapter. See whether you can answer these questions about them.

1. Both *classification* and *analysis* explain things. How are they different? How can we tell whether we have a paper of classification or a paper of analysis?

2. What two things should be clearly stated in a *main idea sentence* for a paper of analysis?

3. What does *operational analysis* do? Is the main idea sentence for a paper of operational analysis usually in the form of a generalization or a specific statement?

4. What does *causal analysis* do? Is the main idea sentence for a paper of causal analysis usually in the form of a generalization or a specific statement?

5. What is the difference between a paper of *operational analysis* and a paper *giving directions?*

6. What is the difference between a paper of *causal analysis* and an *argument?*

Vocabulary

The vocabulary words are given here in sentences similar to or the same as those used in the chapter. Select the meaning that fits the context best.

1. You can explain how a *carburetor* works.
   (a) a device for carbonating water
   (b) a device for mixing gasoline and air
   (c) part of the power brake system
   (d) a device for heating a car _____

2. That *jet* regulates the proper proportion of gas and air.
   (a) an air propelled airplane
   (b) forceful spout of water
   (c) a nozzle
   (d) a faucet _____

3. That jet *regulates* the proper proportion of gas and air.
   (a) restrains
   (b) controls
   (c) rules
   (d) inhibits _____

4. That jet regulates the proper *proportion* of gas and air.
   (a) relative amount
   (b) suitable heat
   (c) proposition
   (d) right direction _____

5. You can explain how blood *courses* through the human body.
   (a) moves in a prescribed direction
   (b) shifts back and forth
   (c) advances from one condition to the next
   (d) undergoes a series of tests _____

6. Analyze the parts of the *circulatory* system.
   (a) round
   (b) oval
   (c) motion of blood to and from the heart
   (d) checking out and returning library books _____

7. A proposal can be *transformed* into state law.
   (a) changed from one condition to another
   (b) shortened in form
   (c) put into legal language
   (d) made to result in electricity _____

8. The anti-dog people *lobbied* for it.
   (a) sat in the balcony and applauded
   (b) tried to persuade law-makers
   (c) bribed the doorkeeper
   (d) threw small paper pellets at the law-makers _____

9. Such explanations are often called *operational* analysis.
   (a) an argument for some operation
   (b) directions on how to make an incision
   (c) why something works
   (d) how something works _____

10. You must pay a singer and an *accompanist*.
    (a) piano player
    (b) a musician who plays an accordion
    (c) organ player
    (d) a musician who assists another performer _____

11. Many people thought dry feet were more important than a new *municipal* swimming pool.
    (a) owned by the city
    (b) full Olympic size
    (c) for children only
    (d) elaborate and expensive _____

12. It would probably decrease the amount of money spent on juvenile *detention* homes.
    (a) for orphans
    (b) for deaf-mutes
    (c) for confining people
    (d) for fixing teeth _____

13. Both operational and *causal* analysis explain something by examining the separate parts.
    (a) careless, informal
    (b) unpremeditated
    (c) why something happens
    (d) how something happens _____

14. Analysis can *range* from the very simple to the very complex.
    (a) occur only out of doors
    (b) occur only in the kitchen
    (c) offer the full scope
    (d) go as if seeking for food   _____

15. It becomes *progressively* complicated as more elements are introduced.
    (a) favoring reforms and changes
    (b) proceeding gradually, step by step
    (c) having to do with social or historical progress
    (d) increased tax rate   _____

16. The difficulties are relative to the *complexity* of the situation.
    (a) complication
    (b) age
    (c) legality
    (d) coloring of the face and skin   _____

17. The paper does not *maintain* that the janitor charged too much.
    (a) establish
    (b) argue
    (c) prove
    (d) preserve   _____

18. His death can be *attributed* to four causes.
    (a) prevented by
    (b) slowed down by
    (c) an occasion of great praise
    (d) assigned to   _____

19. The notion of a *function* or a process is either stated or implied.
    (a) a formal party
    (b) an informal social gathering
    (c) a specific activity
    (d) a mathematical quantity   _____

20. In each of them the whole is a single event, not a *recurring* process.
    (a) happening over and over
    (b) happening only in the past
    (c) erroncous
    (d) careless   _____

Comprehension

Answer this multiple choice quiz according to what is said in the chapter, whether or not it agrees with your own opinion. Sometimes there is more than one right answer; if so, use the letters for *all* the right answers. Sometimes there will be *no* right answer; if so, write "none" in the blank provided.

1. Analysis means
   (a) defining several things in the same paper
   (b) comparing at least four things at the same time
   (c) classifying a special kind of topic
   (d) explaining a whole thing by examining it piece by piece
   (e) telling somebody how to operate something

   _____

2. Although both classification and analysis deal with separate things that somehow belong together,
   (a) classification usually subdivides, labels each subdivision, then sub-divides again
   (b) classification usually tears something down and explains how it goes back together again
   (c) analysis often examines the separate working parts of a single thing
   (d) analysis often shows why one thing is better than another
   (e) analysis often examines the separate causes of a single event

   _____

3. Which of the following topics would be suitable for a paper of analysis?
   (a) the various problems that cause cars to break down
   (b) the working parts of an internal combustion engine
   (c) violent and nonviolent movies
   (d) types of nonviolent movies
   (e) reasons your car wouldn't start yesterday

   _____

4. Operational analysis
   (a) tells you how to operate something
   (b) explains how something works
   (c) applies to mechanical things only
   (d) is concerned with whether a thing *should* happen in a particular way
   (e) applies to either mechanical things or to processes

   _____

5. Causal analysis differs from operational analysis because causal analysis
   (a) concentrates on how something works
   (b) concentrates on why something happened
   (c) deals with a process that works the same way over and over again
   (d) deals with a single event or two or three similar events
   (e) looks to the past rather than to the present
   (f) looks to the present and the future rather than to the past

   _____

6. Main idea sentences for papers of analysis
   (a) usually have two parts
   (b) need only say what is being analyzed
   (c) sometimes show what the whole is and say what parts make up the whole
   (d) sometimes show what the whole is and how many parts make up the whole
   (c) usually indicate whether the analysis will be operational or causal

   _____

7. The order of a paper of analysis
   (a) is sometimes indicated by the main idea sentence
   (b) is never indicated by the main idea sentence
   (c) can move from what happened first to what happened next
   (d) can move from least important cause to most important cause
   (e) should always be arranged according to time

   _____

8. Which of these main idea sentences would be suitable for operational analysis?
   (a) There were four main reasons for the founding of Resurrection City.
   (b) The failure of Congress to provide more food for starving Americans is the shame of our time.
   (c) A bill becomes law only after Congress has passed it through several stages.
   (d) According to a recent television survey, ten million Americans cannot afford enough to eat.
   (e) In 1968, Americans spent more money on cigarettes than was distributed in surplus food.

   _____

9. Which of these main idea sentences would be suitable for causal analysis?
   (a) There were four main reasons for the founding of Resurrection City.
   (b) The failure of Congress to provide more food for starving Americans is the shame of our time.
   (c) A bill becomes law only after Congress has passed it through several stages.
   (d) According to a recent television survey, ten million Americans cannot afford enough to eat.
   (e) In 1968, Americans spent more money on cigarettes than was distributed in surplus food.

   _____